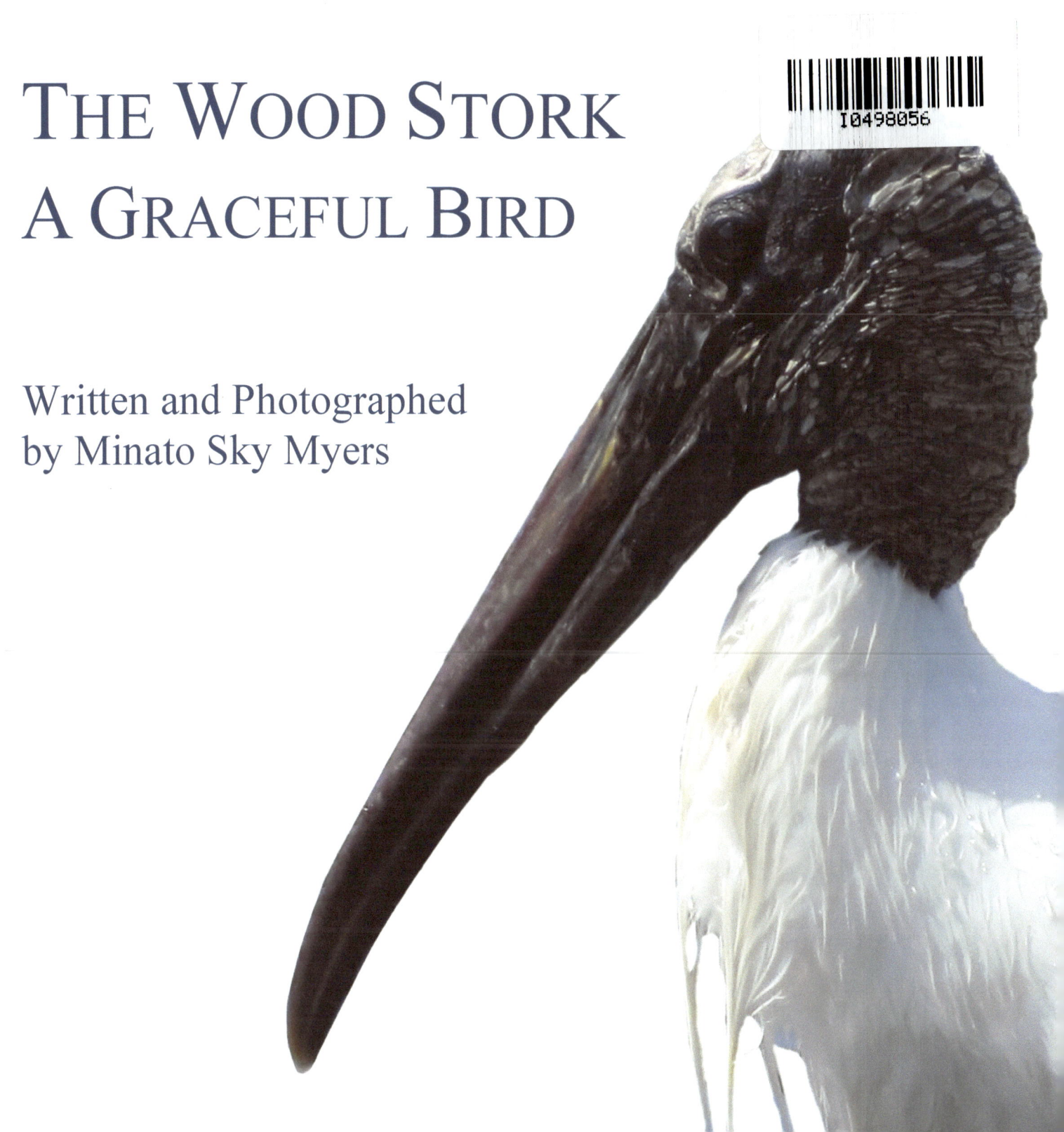

The Wood Stork
A Graceful Bird

Written and Photographed
by Minato Sky Myers

The Wood Stork: A Graceful Bird by Minato Sky Myers

Published by Minato Sky Myers

4581 Weston Road #165, Weston, FL 33331-3141 USA

Copyright © 2018 Minato Sky Myers

All photographs copyright © 2018 Minato Sky Myers

All rights reserved. No portion of this book may be reproduced in any form without permission from the publisher, except as permitted by U.S. copyright law.

Cover by Minato Sky Myers

ISBN 13 978-1722781583

ISBN 10 1722781580

"You can't conserve what you haven't got."

— Marjory Stoneman Douglas

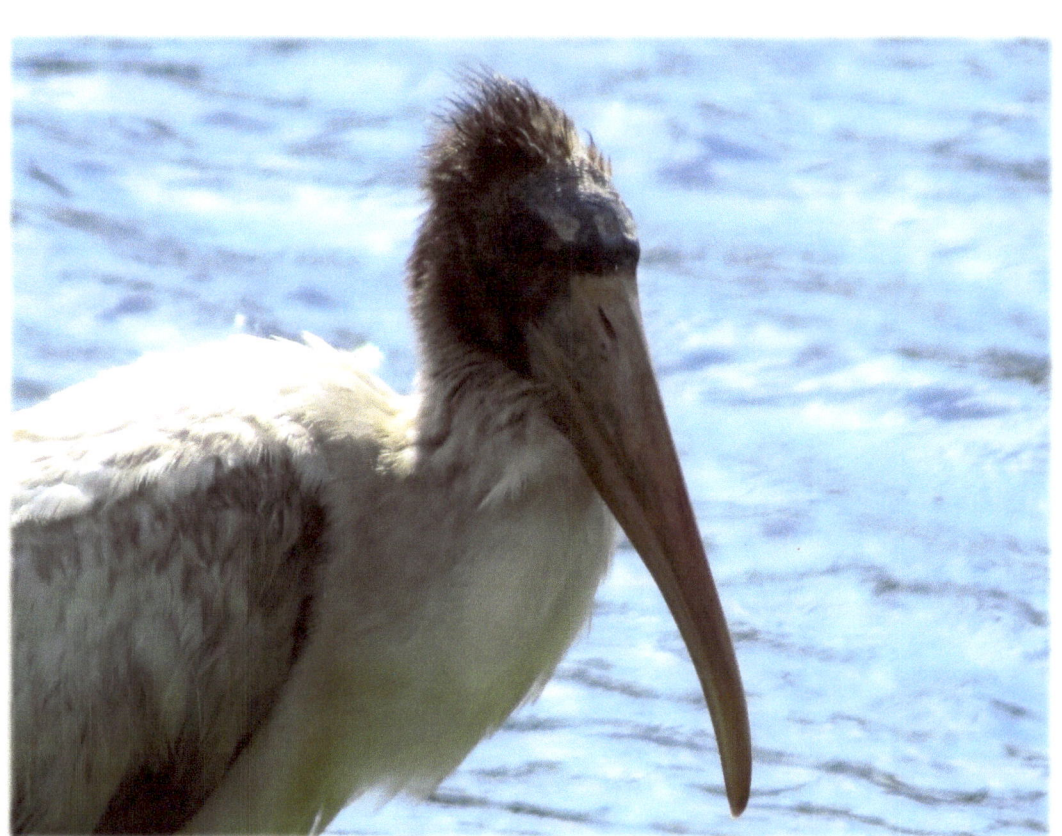

Contents

Introduction	1
Habitat	4
Foraging	5
Nest Building	7
Competition	8
Displays	11
Pairing	13
Nestlings	14
Feeding	16
Growing Up	18
Dancing	23
Conservation	24
References	26

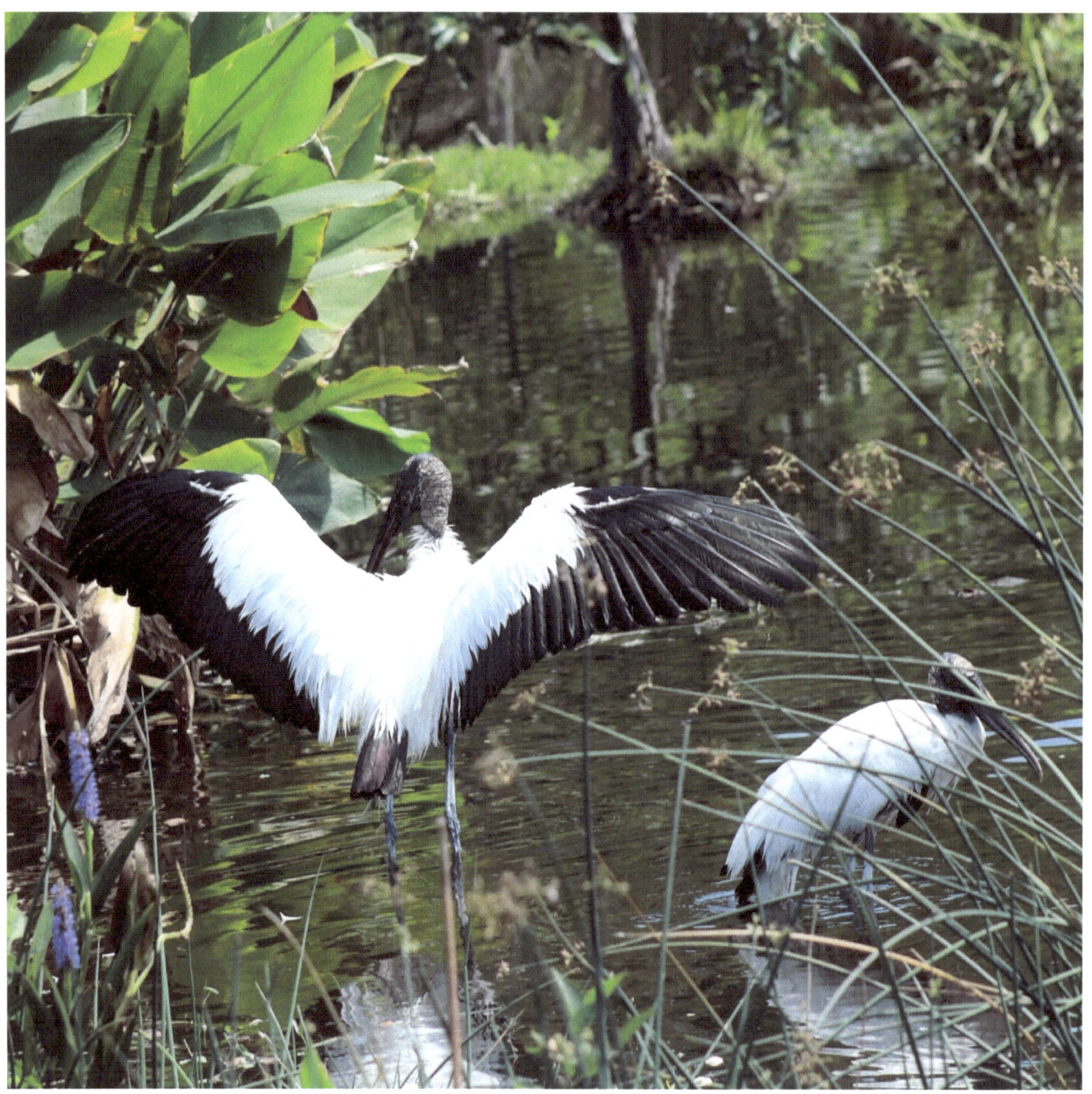

WOOD STORKS are large wading birds indigenous to the Americas. Their scientific name is *Mycteria americana* and they were formerly called "wood ibises." The storks stand about a meter tall, with white plumage, black, iridescent wing tips, and a bald, featherless head and neck. To feed, wood storks forage in shallow, murky water, feeling for fish. They also consume crustaceans, frogs, salamanders, small snakes, and even baby alligators. When prey touches their long, sharp beaks, they shut their beaks tight and tilt their heads back to swallow it whole. This reflex is one of the fastest among all birds.

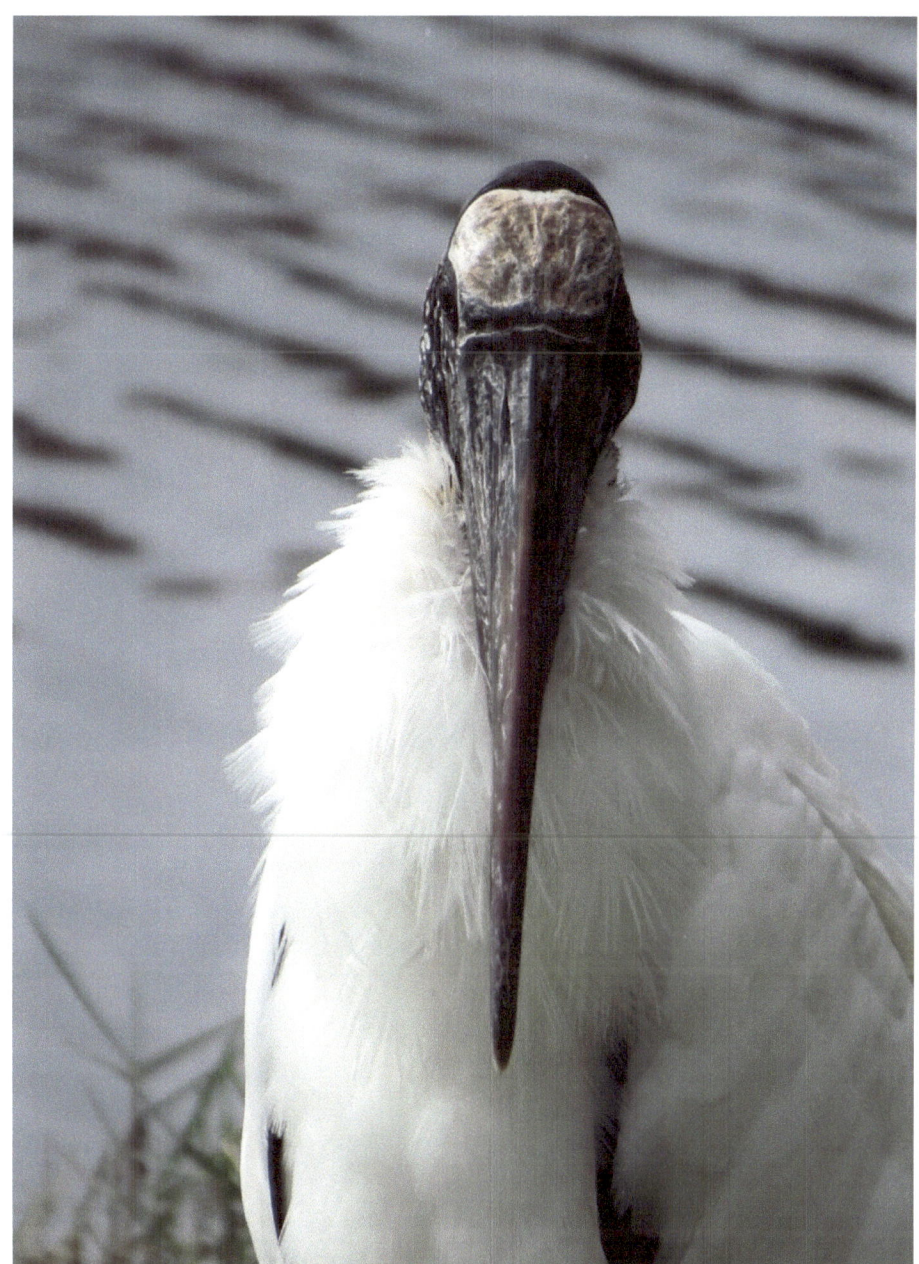

Wood storks are the only storks that breed in North America, mainly in the Carolinas, Georgia, Florida and the Yucatan. They build their nests in trees surrounded by shallow water. In courtship, males are hostile to females at first, but preen them and offer sticks once arguments settle. The cream-colored eggs are around two and a half inches in length and incubate over a period of 28 to 32 days. Once hatched, the young need 60 to 65 days to become able to feed independently.

South Florida is also home to dozens of other wading bird species, such as great blue herons, great egrets, reddish egrets, green herons, white ibis, cattle egrets, and even the occasional spoonbill. Their plumage, especially in breeding season, is so beautiful that they were almost hunted to extinction in the early 20th century to supply the fashion industry. Perhaps the naked, wrinkled head and neck of wood storks kept the fashionistas away, and may have helped their population survive, but habitat loss still put their population at risk.

In Florida, their numbers declined from approximately 60,000 in the 1930s to fewer than 5,000 breeding pairs in the 1980s, and were listed as endangered in 1984. From 1984 to 2004 their U.S. population increased by about 60 percent, leading the U.S. Fish and Wildlife Service to upgrade their status to Threatened. Currently, their global breeding population is 450,000. Still, due to their feeding and nesting habits, small changes in water levels leave wood storks vulnerable to starvation or predation.

To ensure that wood storks will be around for generations to come, it is important to coordinate efforts across multiple agencies. We need to manage water flow in a way that minimizes impact to their population, monitor the population and health of breeding colonies, and preserve wetlands for them to recover. Non-profits like the Audubon Society and The Nature Conservancy purchase and manage land for wood storks and many other native species to thrive. Research from the Audubon Society suggests that artificially managed wetland areas, like those in my city, may be enough to help the breeding populations survive and grow.

Wood storks were the species that inspired me to start taking snapshots of birds. I first encountered them near my backyard, where they have established a perennial breeding colony. I later visited more groups in the Florida Everglades, Corkscrew Swamp Sanctuary, and local sites like Green Cay Nature Center, but my hometown of Weston has been a reliable, year-round source of photos.

The photo below shows what typically happens around here in the late spring. Each year, the wood storks build their nests on an island near the edge of this retention pond, about 20 feet (6 m) above the water. At the height of the season, the branches droop with the weight of birds competing for a spot. Their white feathers illuminate the leaves, reflecting the golden sunlight.

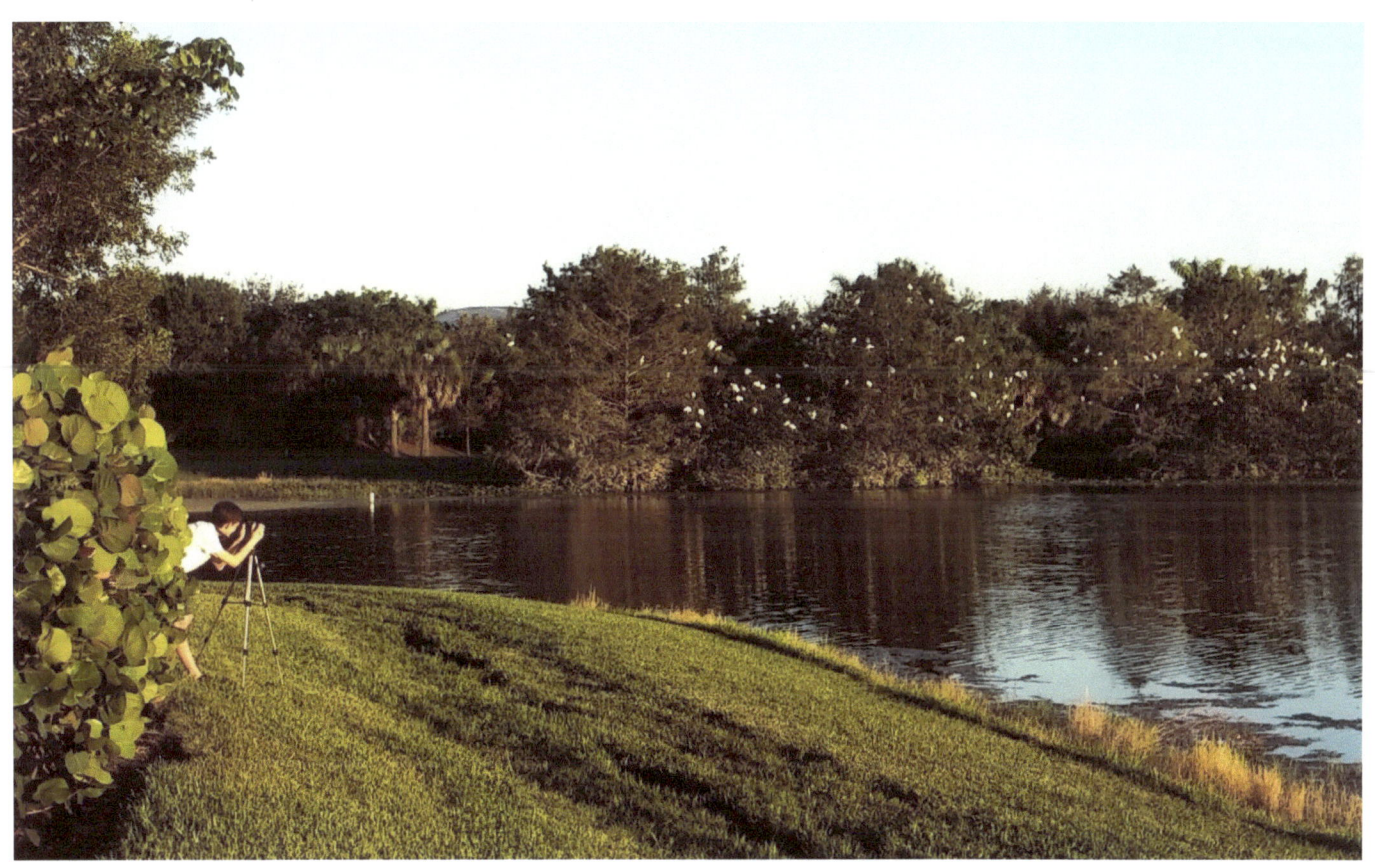

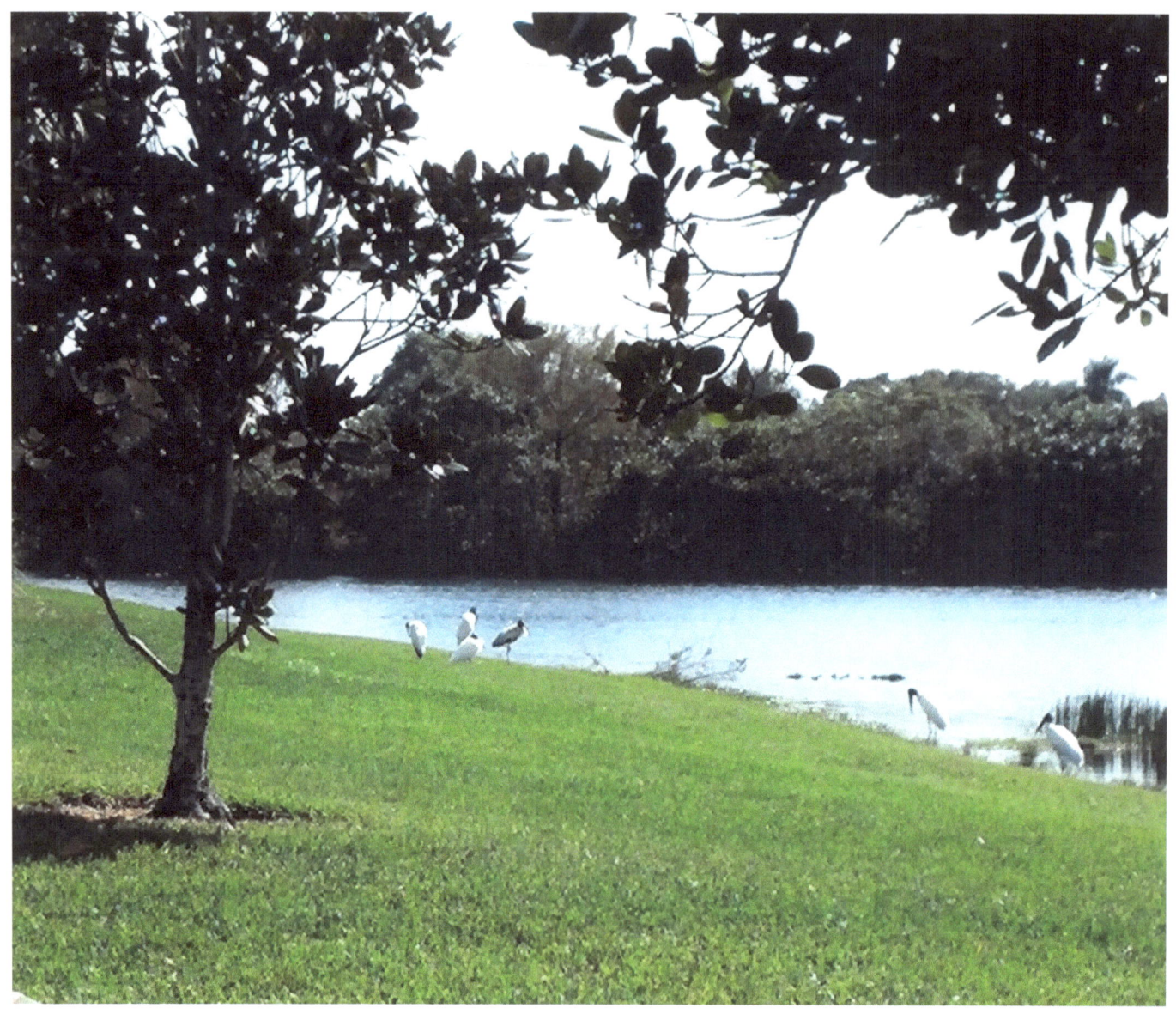

SUBURBAN HABITAT. Historically, wood storks bred in forested wetlands. In the 20th century, they established breeding colonies around artificial ponds like this one in Broward County, Florida. The steady water depth supports their feeding strategy, while nearby trees protect nestlings from predators.

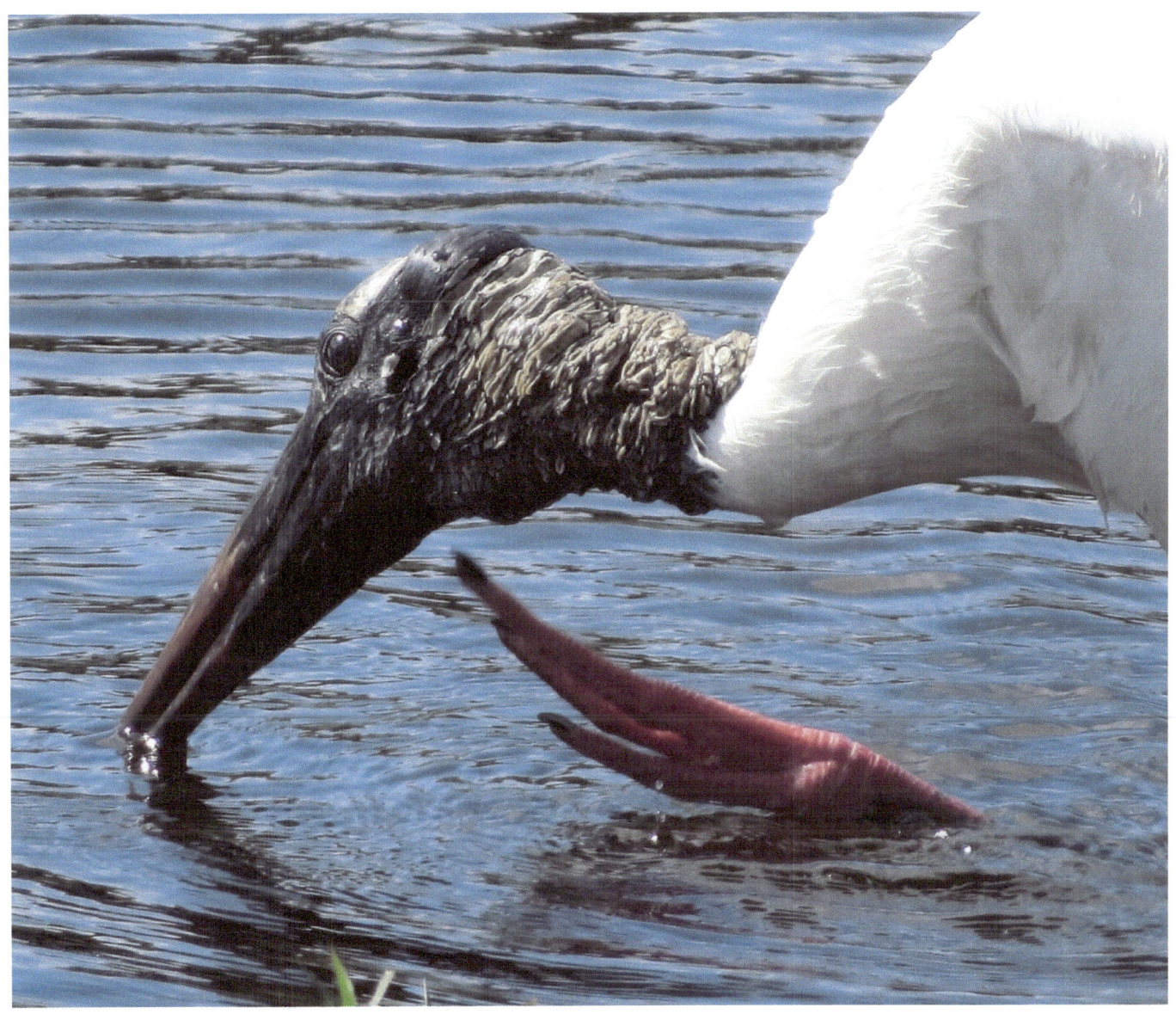

FORAGING. When prey touches their beak, a quick reflex snaps it closed. If the water is too deep, wood storks cannot reach the prey — too shallow, and aquatic prey cannot thrive. Humans have drained, cleared, and mismanaged water, reducing the area in which the storks can successfully forage.

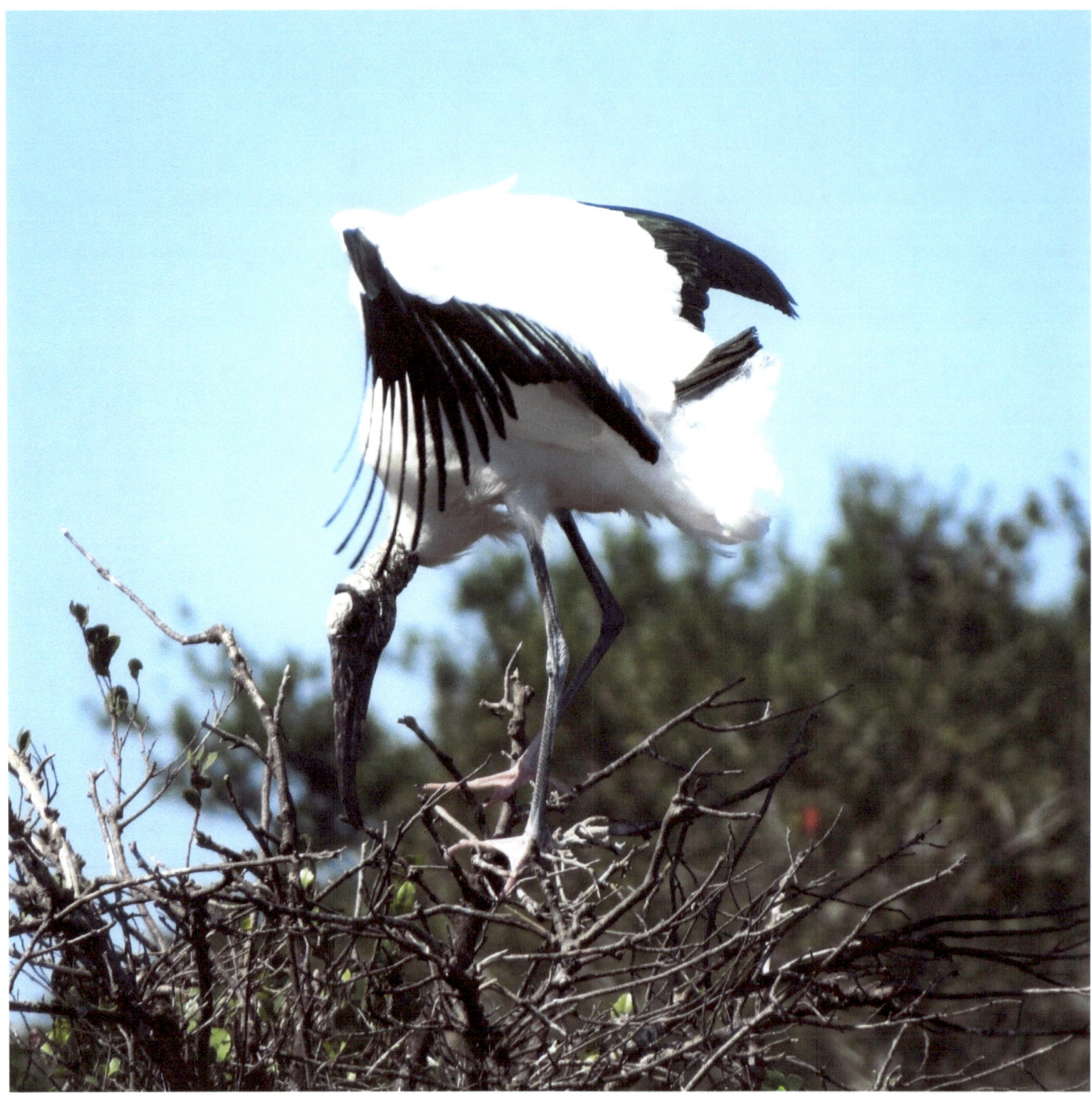

NEST BUILDING. The stork on the opposite page is moving branches around to create a more stable nest. These branches have served as a rookery for wood storks and other birds for decades.

This juvenile (right, top) is looking for a comfortable spot among the branches. Breeding pairs (right, bottom) arrive during the mild winter to stake out space among the leaves: high above the water and away from ground predators. Nesting continues through spring and summer. Wood storks are present every month except September and October. As other wading birds come and go, they compete with the storks for space and food.

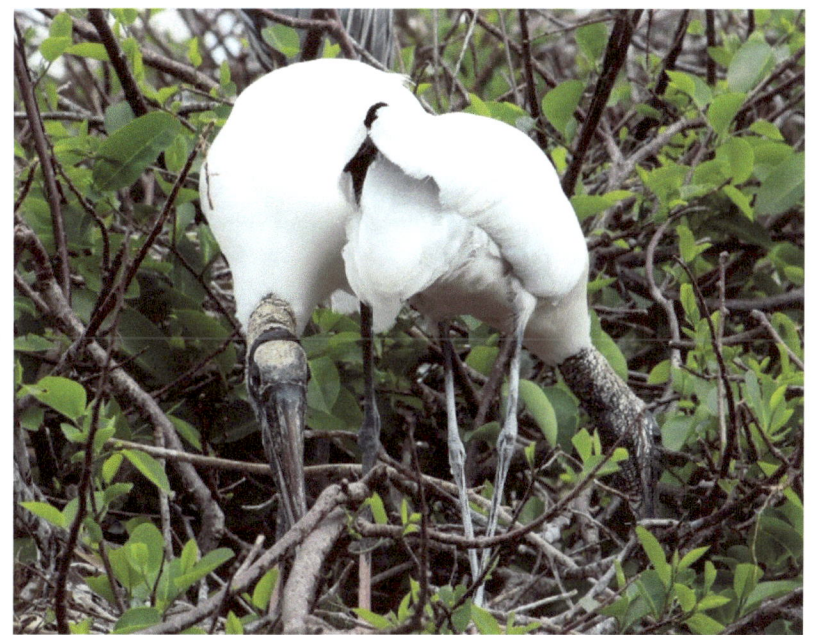

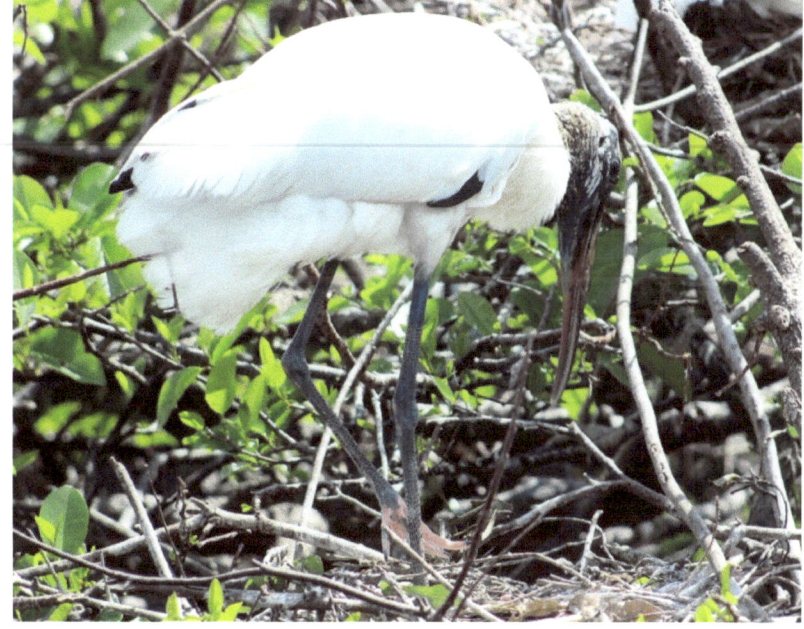

COMPETITION. Life along the shore means sharing with other wading birds and water-associated birds. Here, in Wakodahatchee Wetlands, a wood stork and great cormorant seem to dance together as both raise their wings and circle each other (below). When defending their territory, the storks take on an aggressive posture: they raise their wings, bend their heads down, open their beaks, stare at their opponent, and make a hissing noise. These impressive displays also take place in the tree tops, like the encounter with an anhinga (below, right). By asserting their strength, size, and territorial dominance, wood storks can protect their homes from unwanted visitors.

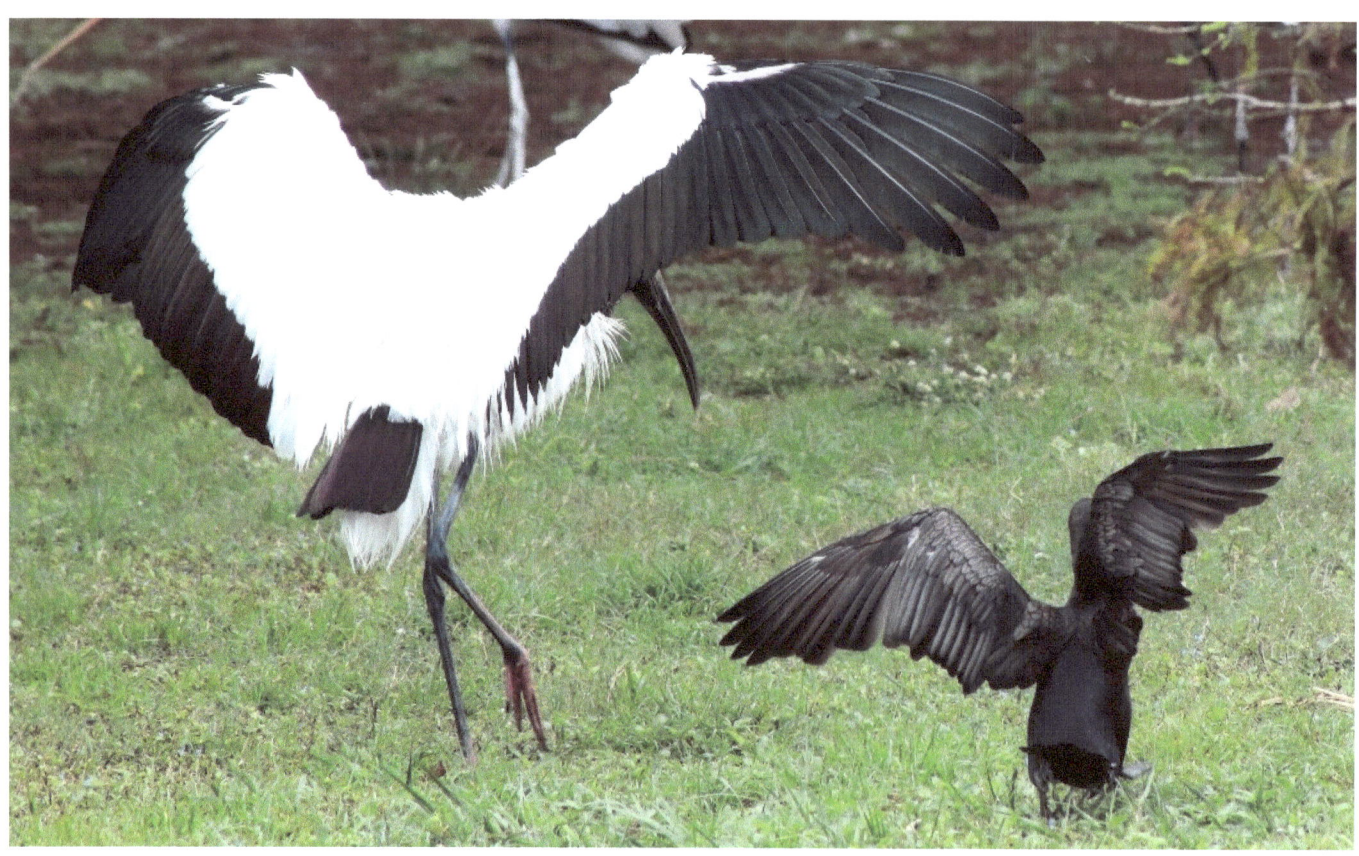

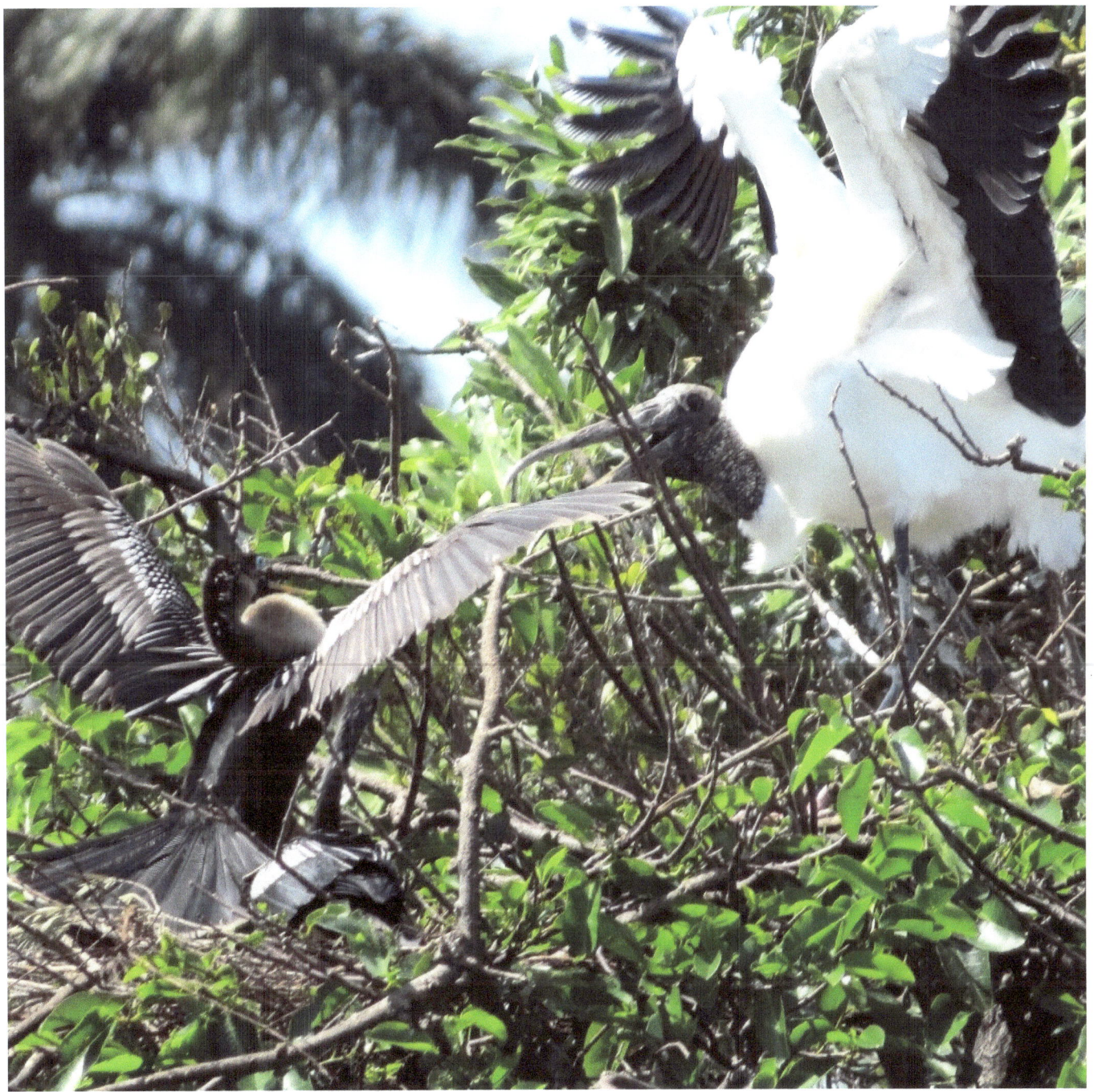

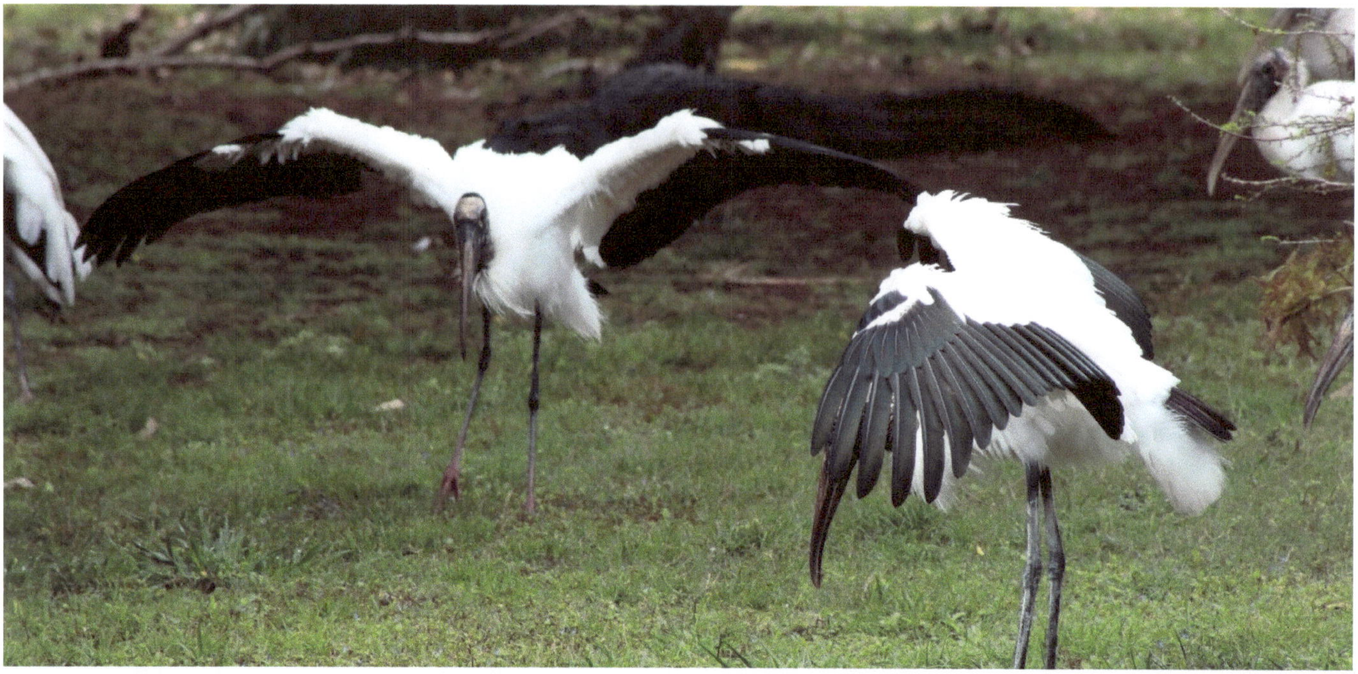

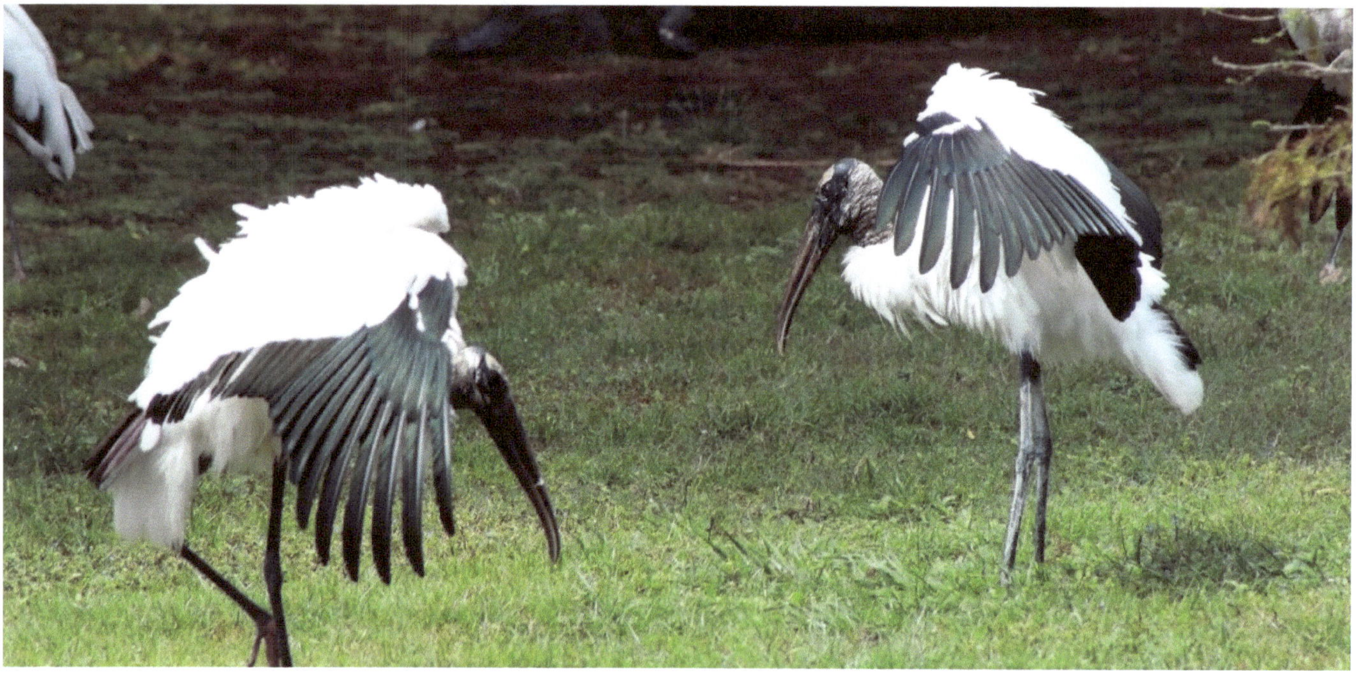

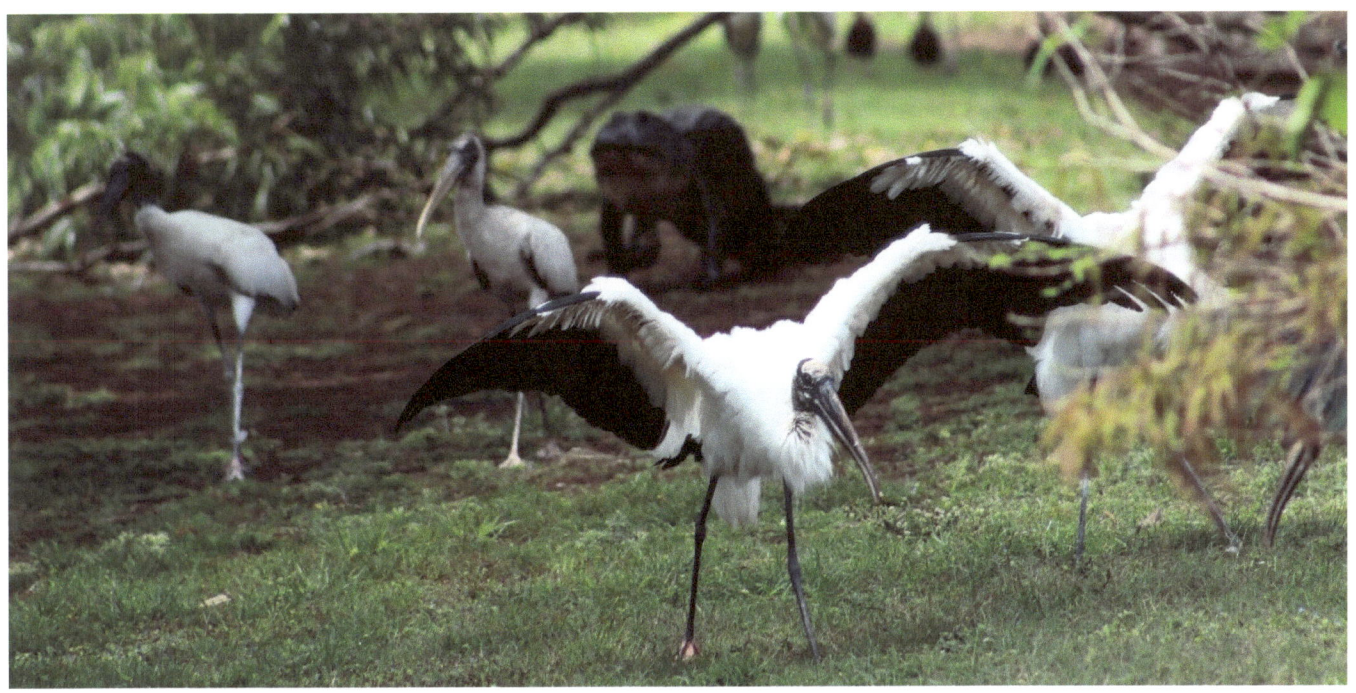

DISPLAYS. This aggressive display started between two adult wood storks standing near a group of pale-billed juveniles (opposite, top). Focused on each other, however, they did not seem to mind the alligator cooling off in the shadows nearby. Once the alligator began to move, the storks took notice and moved to safety, wings still outstretched (opposite, bottom). As the alligator rose and lumbered closer, the birds advanced in a slow-motion game of tag (above).

At over three feet (1 m) in length, wood storks are among the largest wading birds and have few predators. In fact, wood storks strategically nest near alligators to protect the nestlings from territorial animals like raccoons and opossums. Birds of prey, including hawks, vultures, and caracaras, can take the young or eggs. In recent years, the storks have also been threatened by invasive exotic species like the Burmese python.

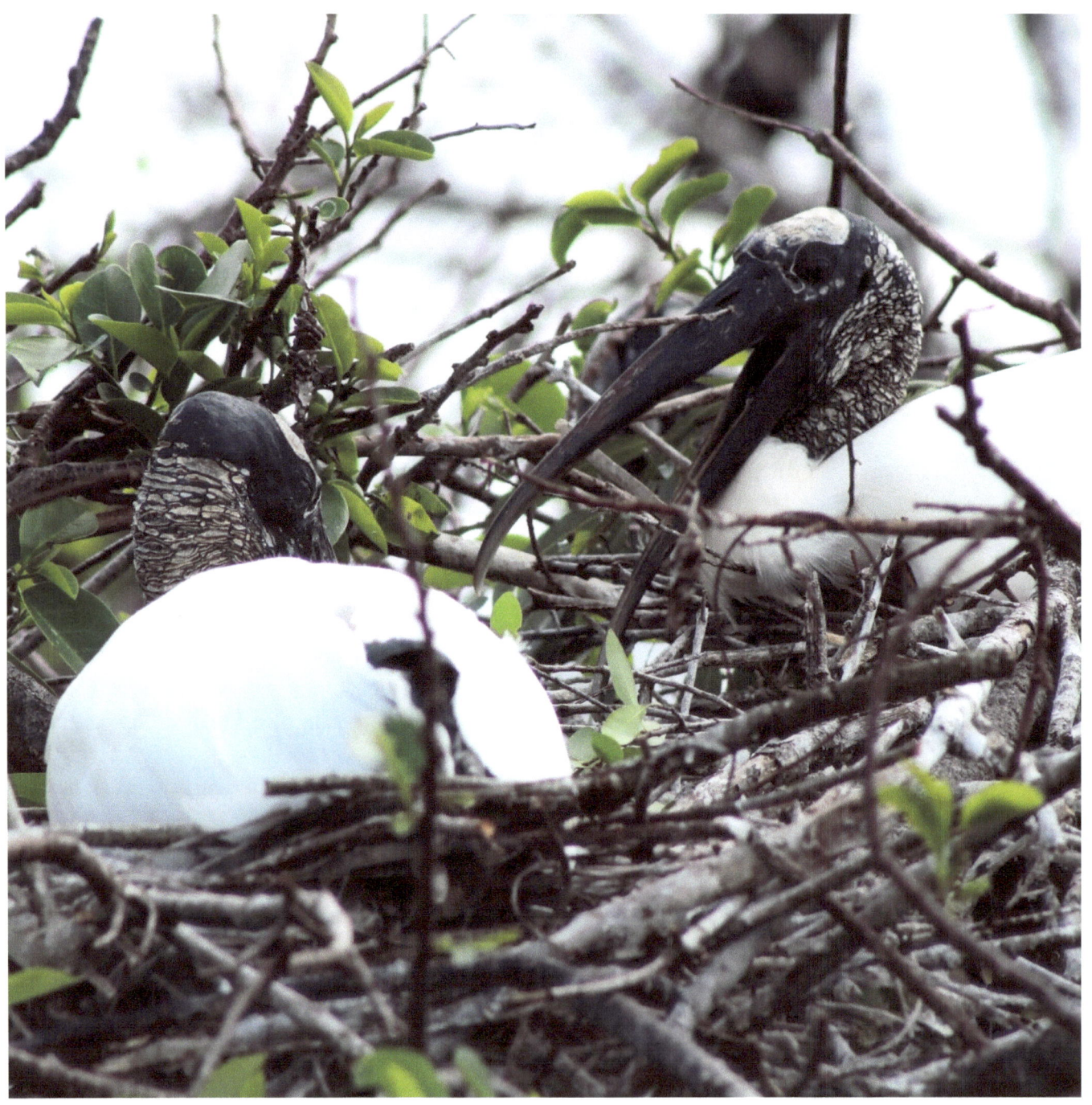

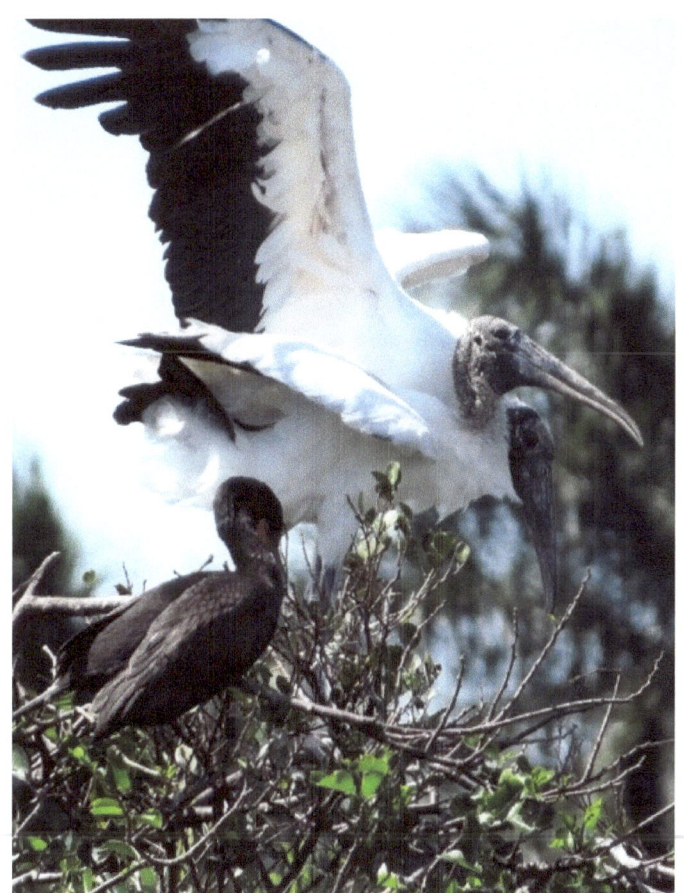 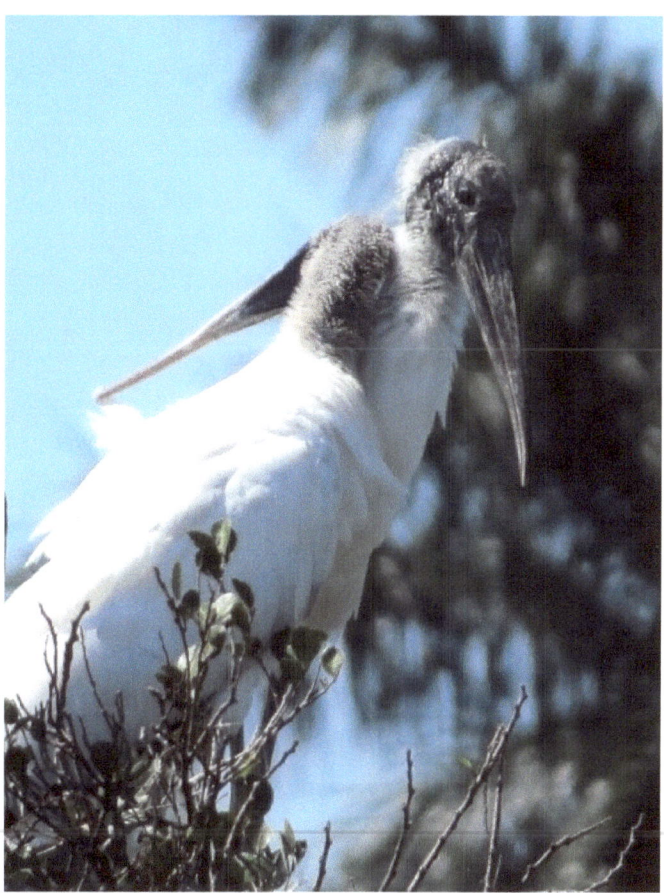

PAIRING. Wood stork pairs often stay together for life. Both the female and the male return year after year to the same colony to maintain the nest. Opposite: A mated pair rest together in their nest. Above: A young couple mate and bond. They seem oblivious to the great cormorant preening nearby. This scene took place in a wood stork nesting colony in Broward County that is home to around 25 nesting pairs each season.

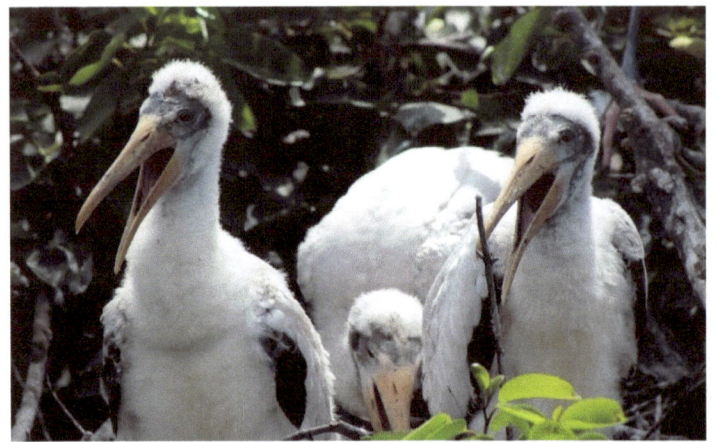
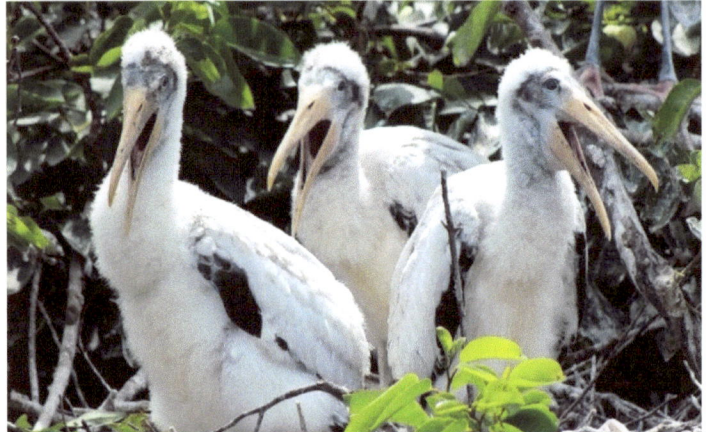
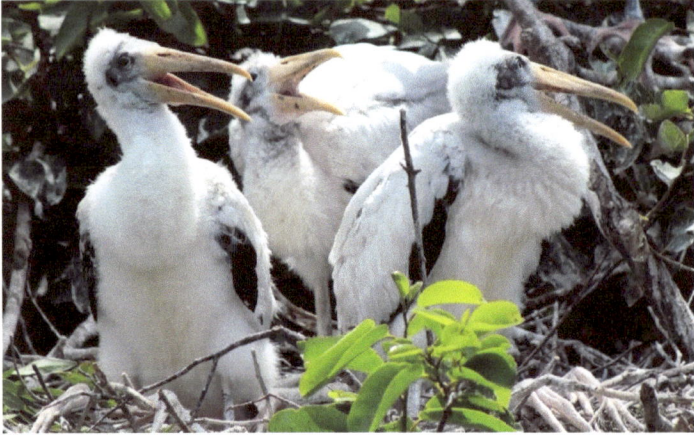

NESTLINGS. Perched in a nest 20 feet (6 m) above the water, a rowdy trio of yellow-beaked juvenile wood storks squawks for food from their parents (left). The young depend on the adults to bring them food for about nine weeks. During this period of rapid growth, they eat about 36 pounds (16 kg) until they can feed independently.

As wood storks develop into adults, their pale beaks darken and the downy white feathers on their heads and necks give way to black and grey wrinkled skin. Opposite: This family group of two adults and four juveniles stayed together throughout the two-month nesting period.

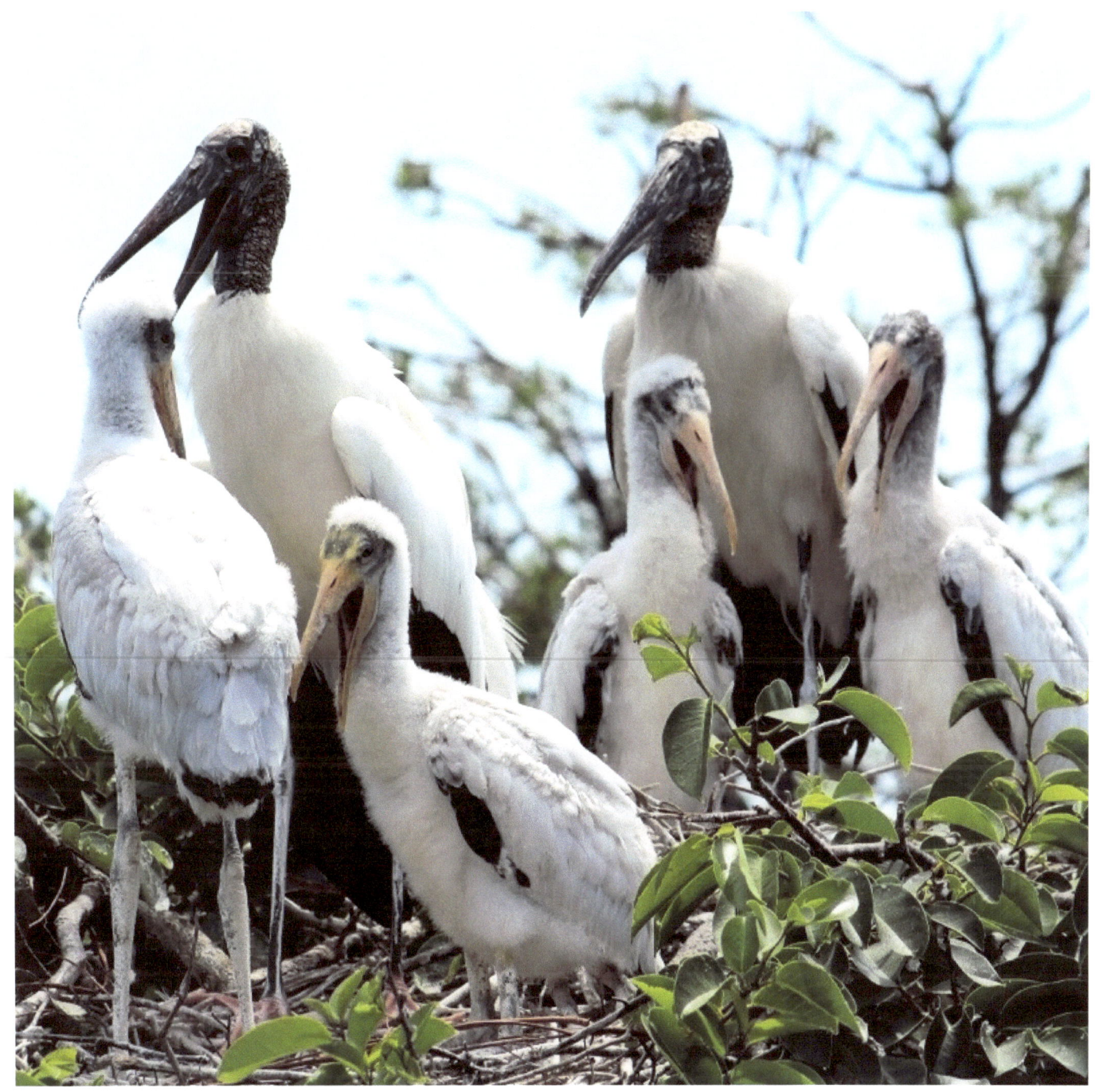

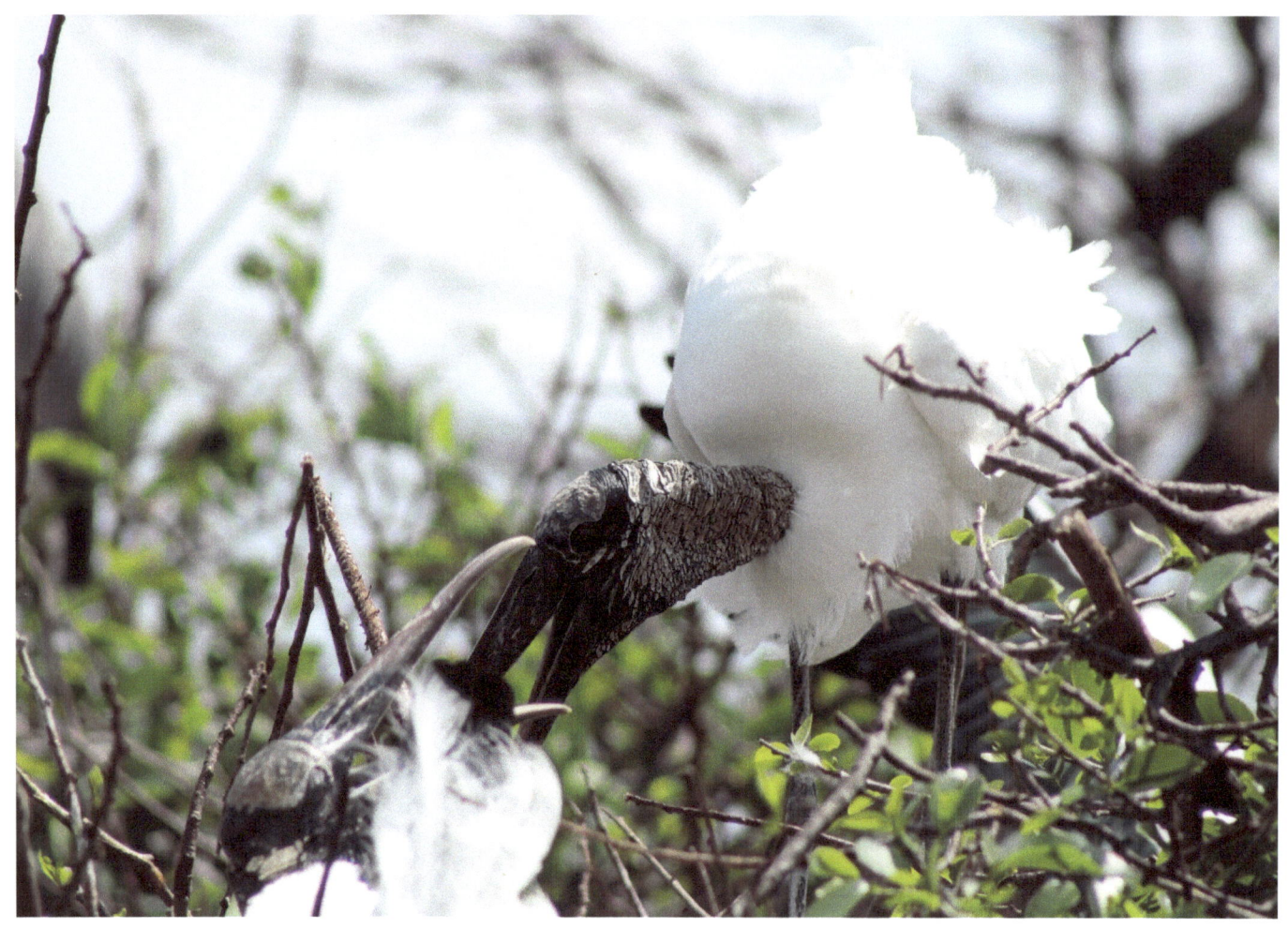

FEEDING. When adults return from foraging, the nestlings interact with their parents and persuade them to provide food. When nestlings are smaller, their parents regurgitate whole fish into the nest (above). As they grow, parents feed the juveniles directly, beak-to-beak. At right, a juvenile is shown stimulating its parent's bill and breast, then preening the parent's feathers. This helps them learn to socialize with other birds and prepare to preen themselves.

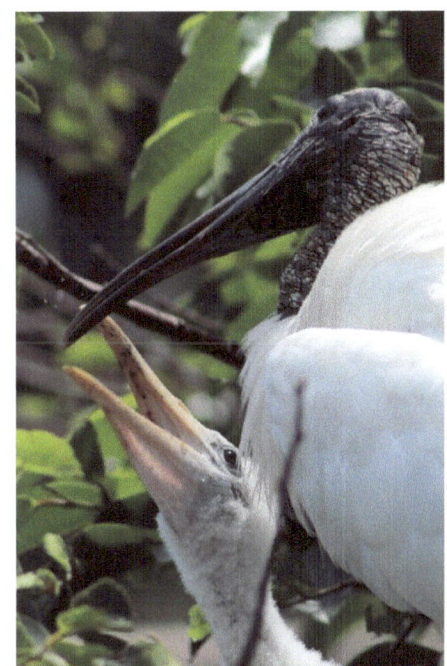 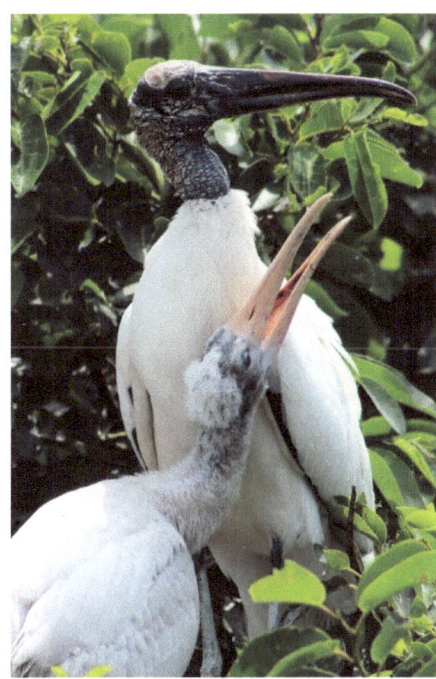 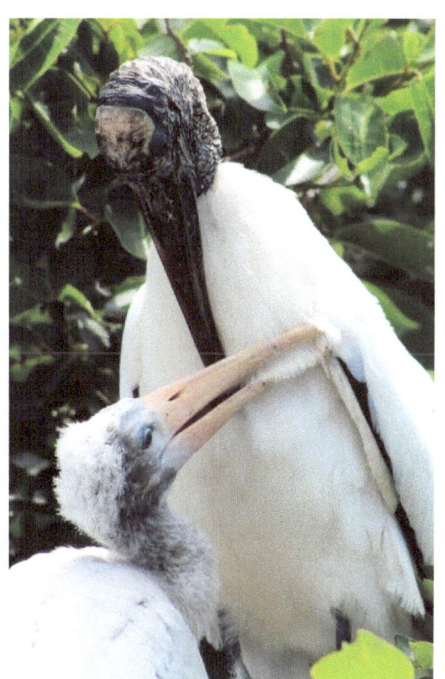

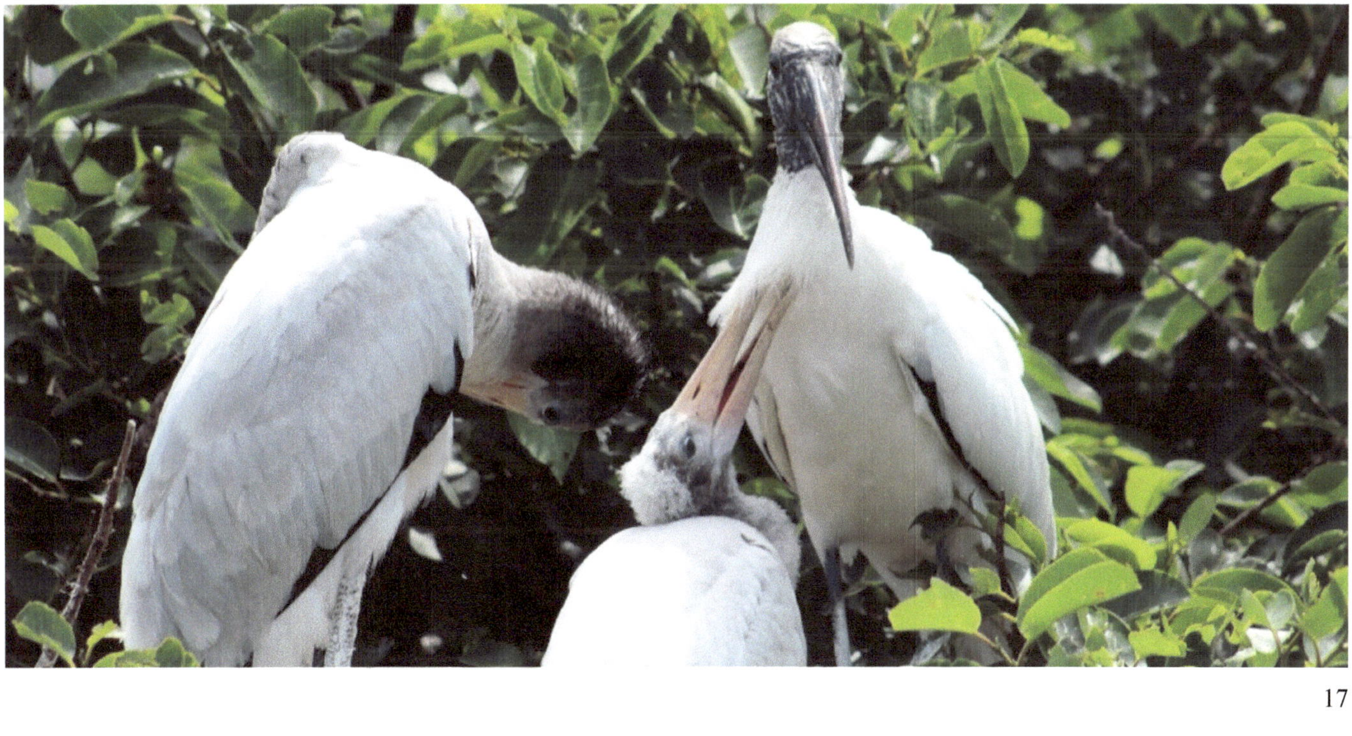

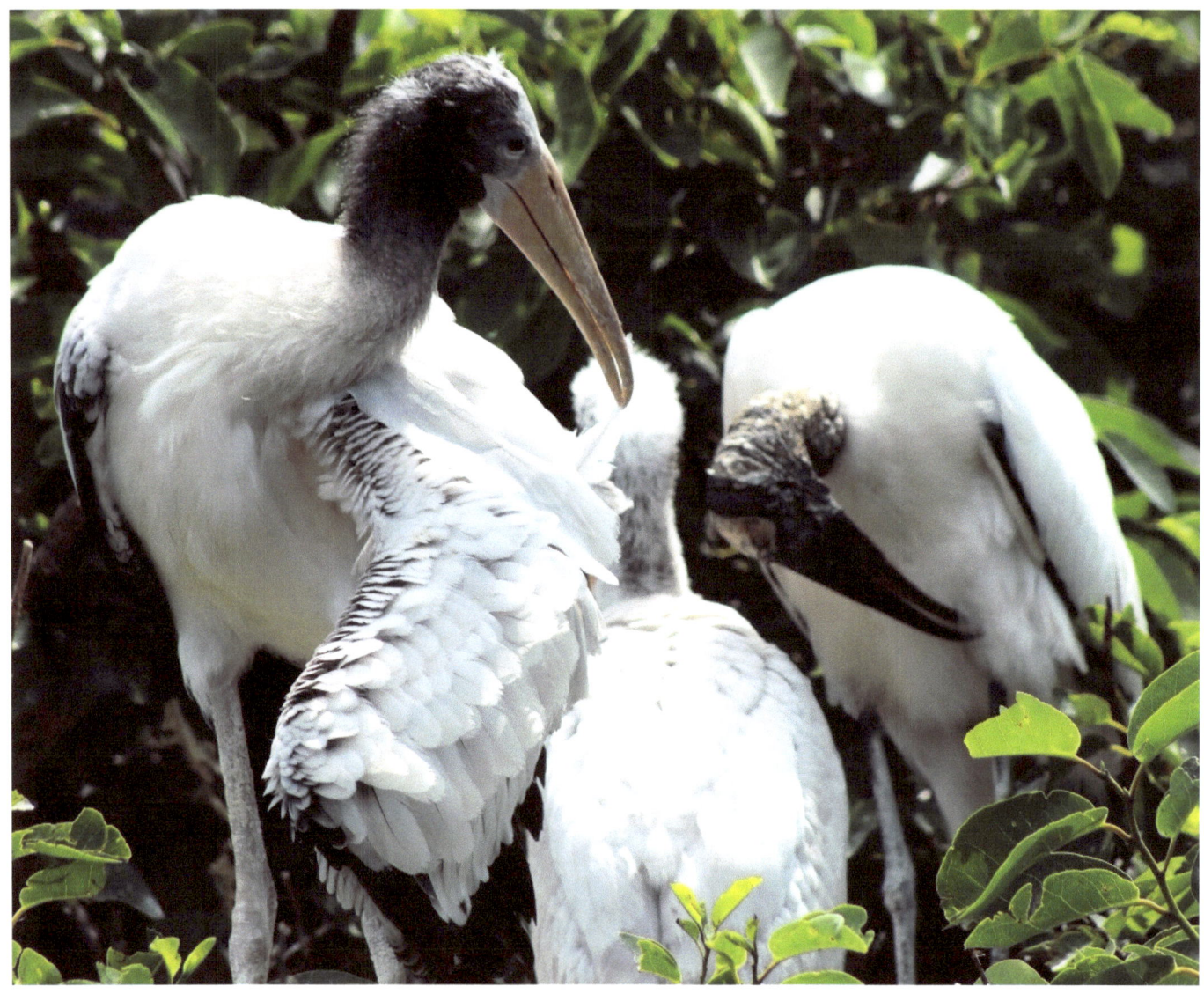

GROWING UP. Wood storks are shown in three stages: a fledgling preening its juvenile plumage (left), a nestling (center), and a mature stork preening its adult plumage (right). Nestlings take flight at seven or eight weeks old, forage independently at about nine weeks, then leave the colony at ten to twelve weeks.

In this close-up, an immature wood stork starts to show signs of adulthood. In this process, the plumage on the head and neck grows darker, and the beak starts to change color.

Like most birds, the wood stork preens itself with oil from its uropygial gland, located on the base of its tail. Juveniles take three to four years to reach full reproductive maturity. The following pages provide a side-by-side comparison of juvenile and adult plumage.

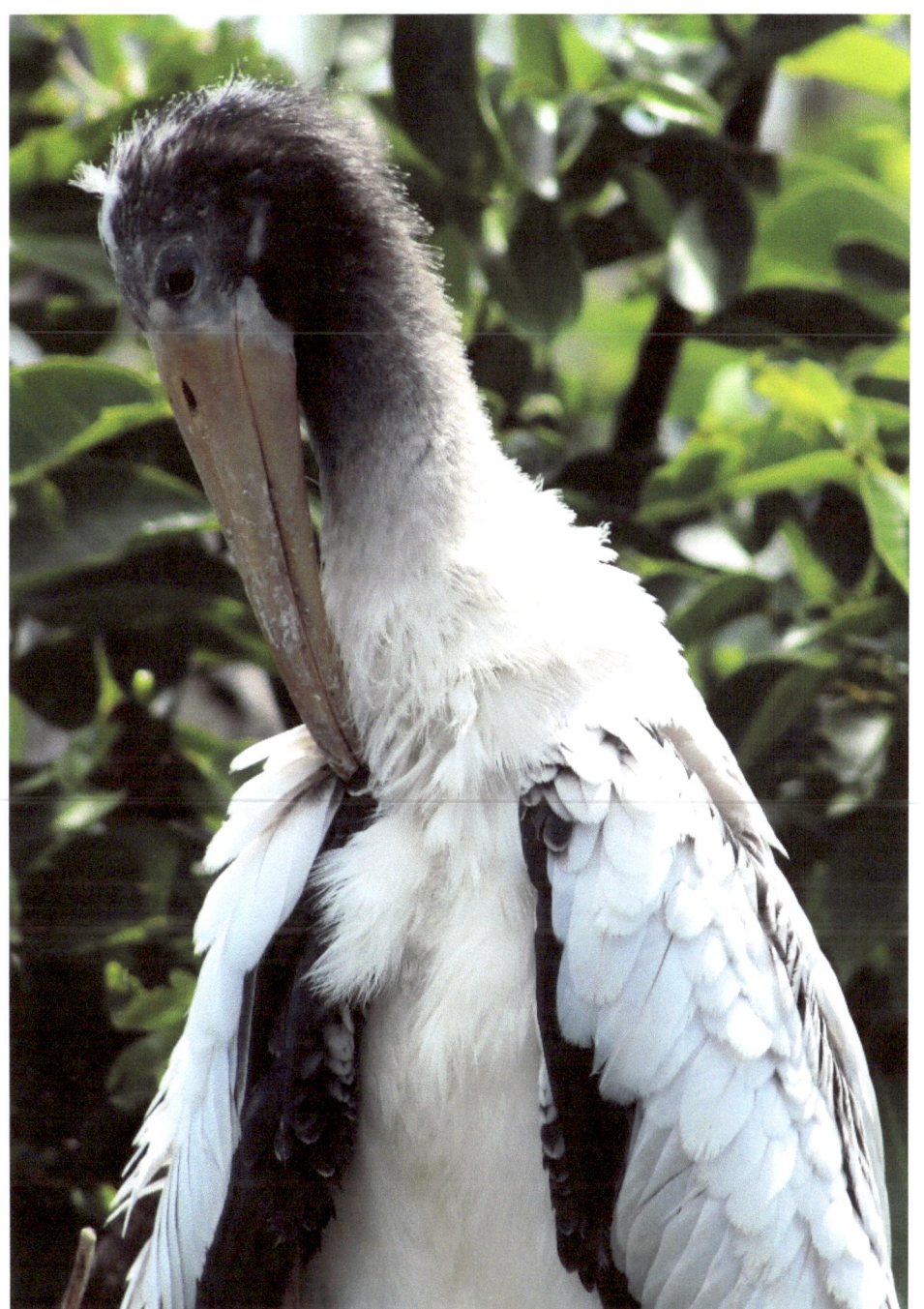

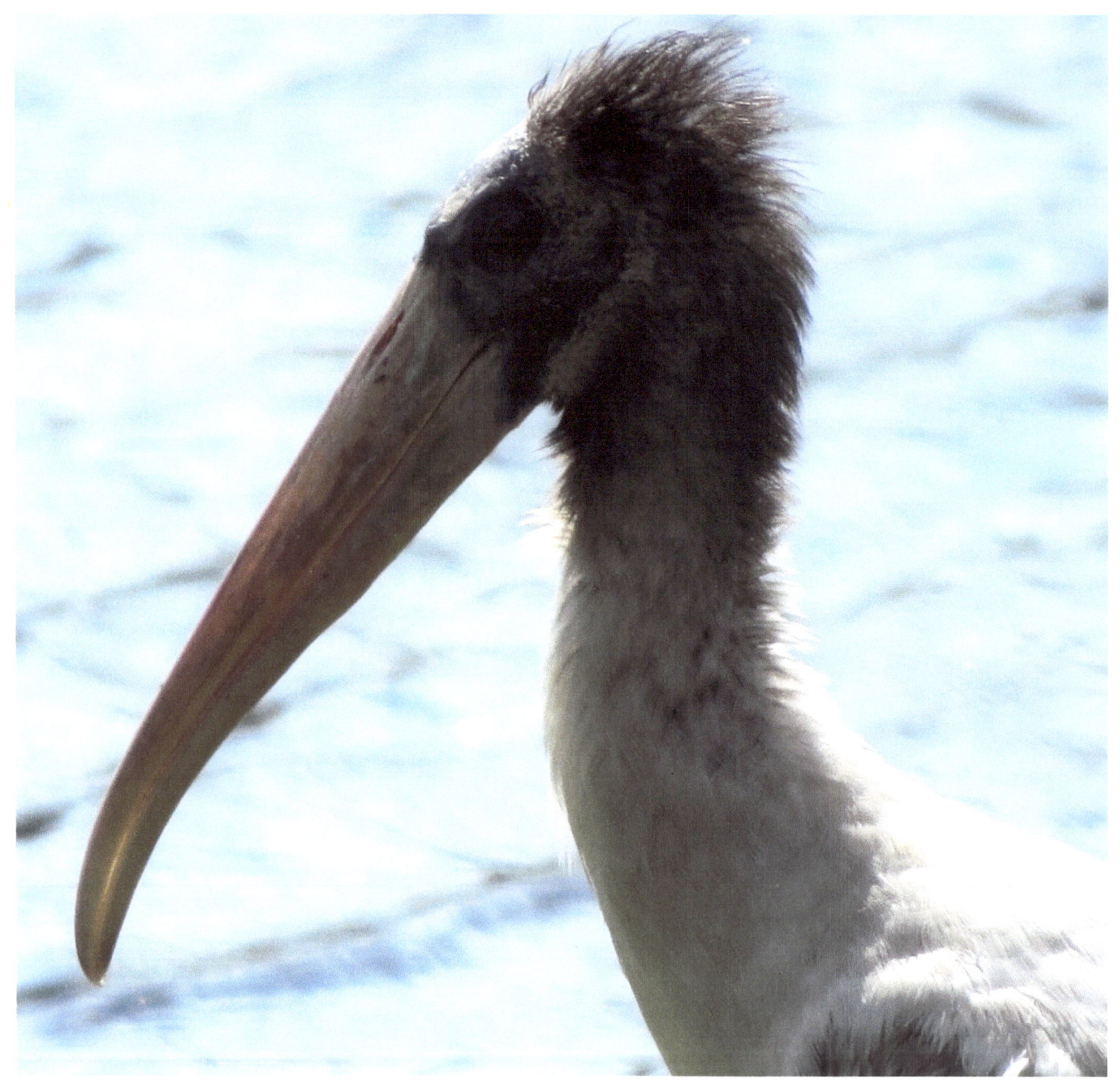

JUVENILE

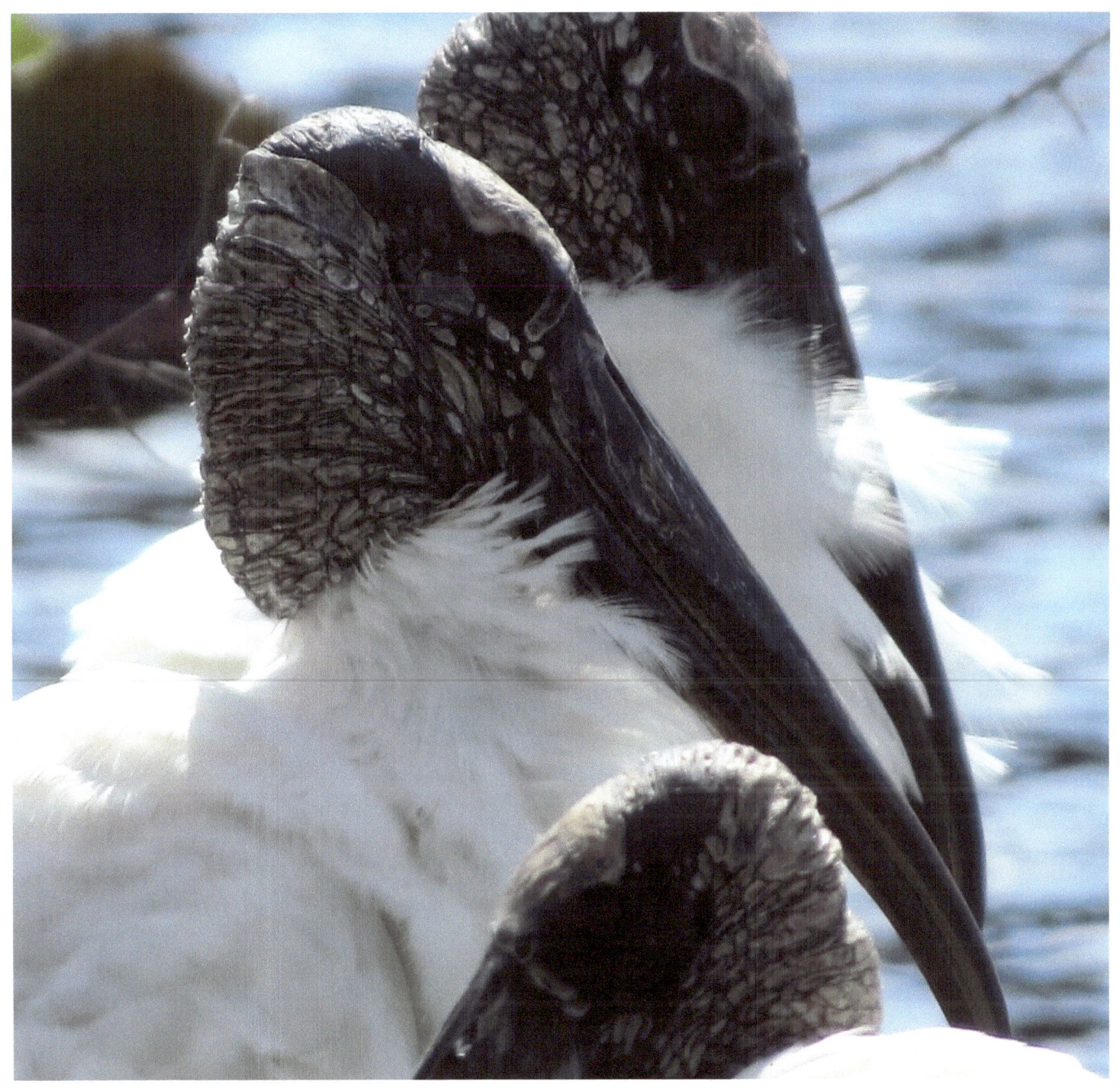
Adults

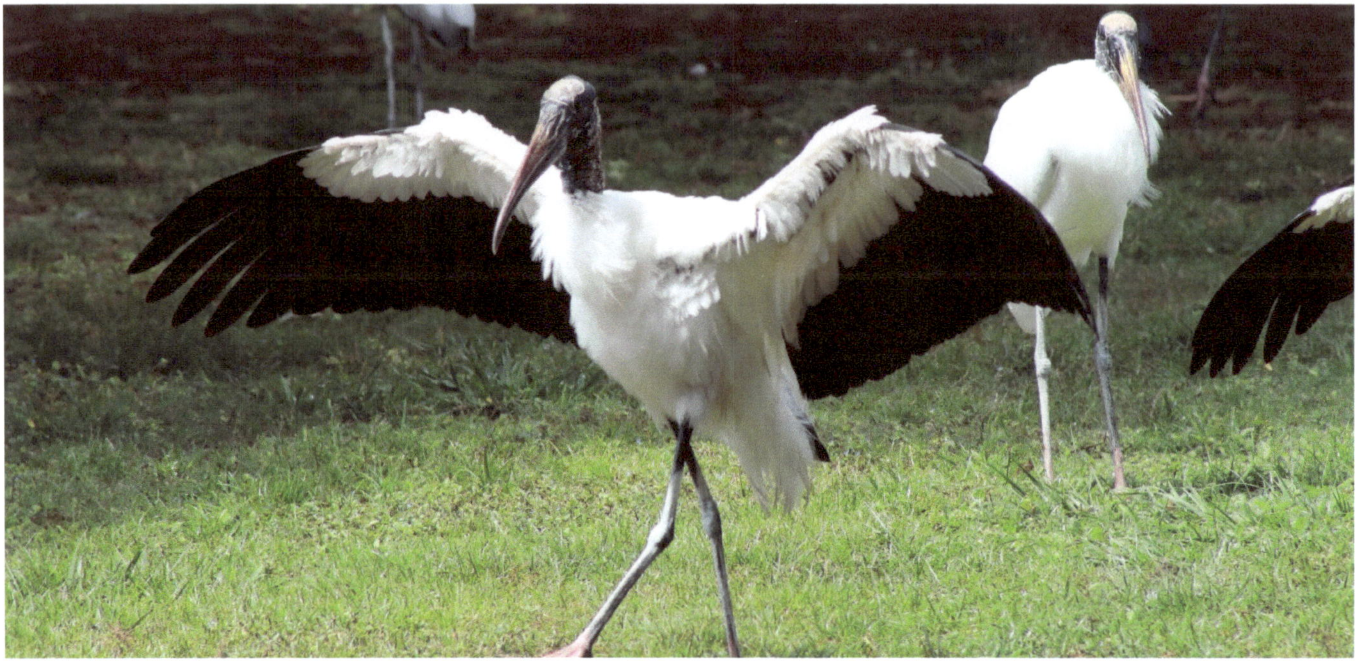

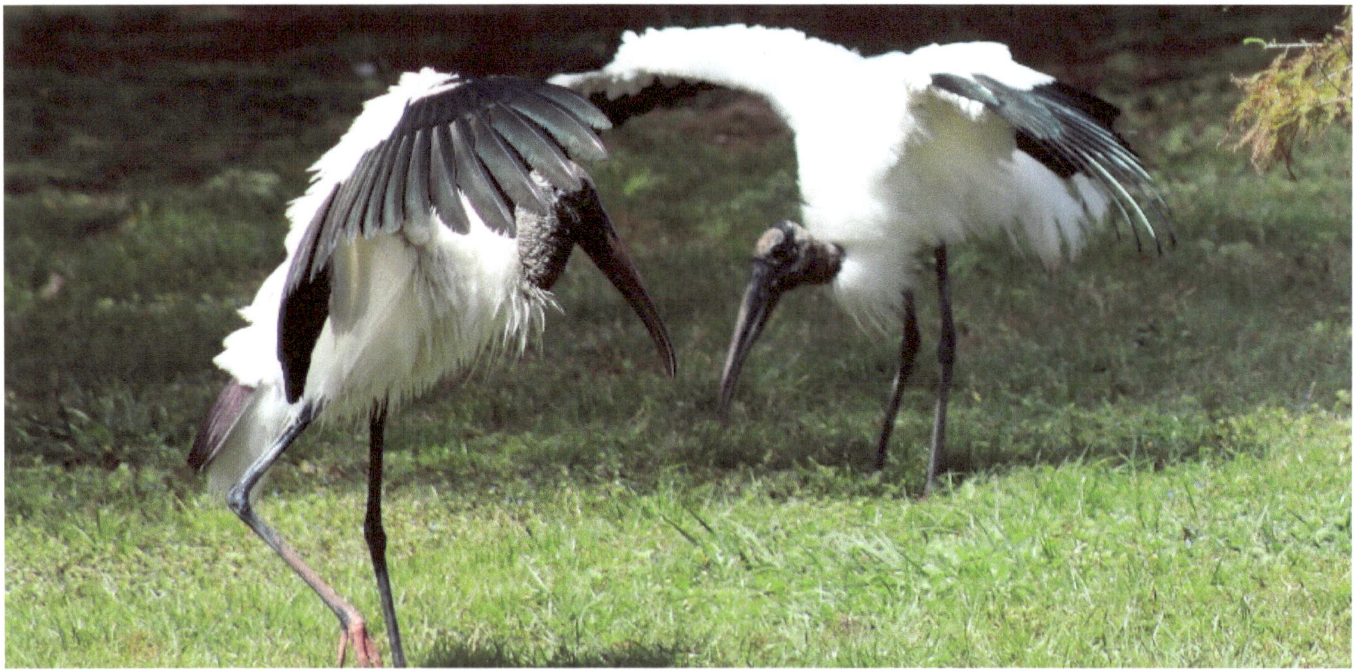

22

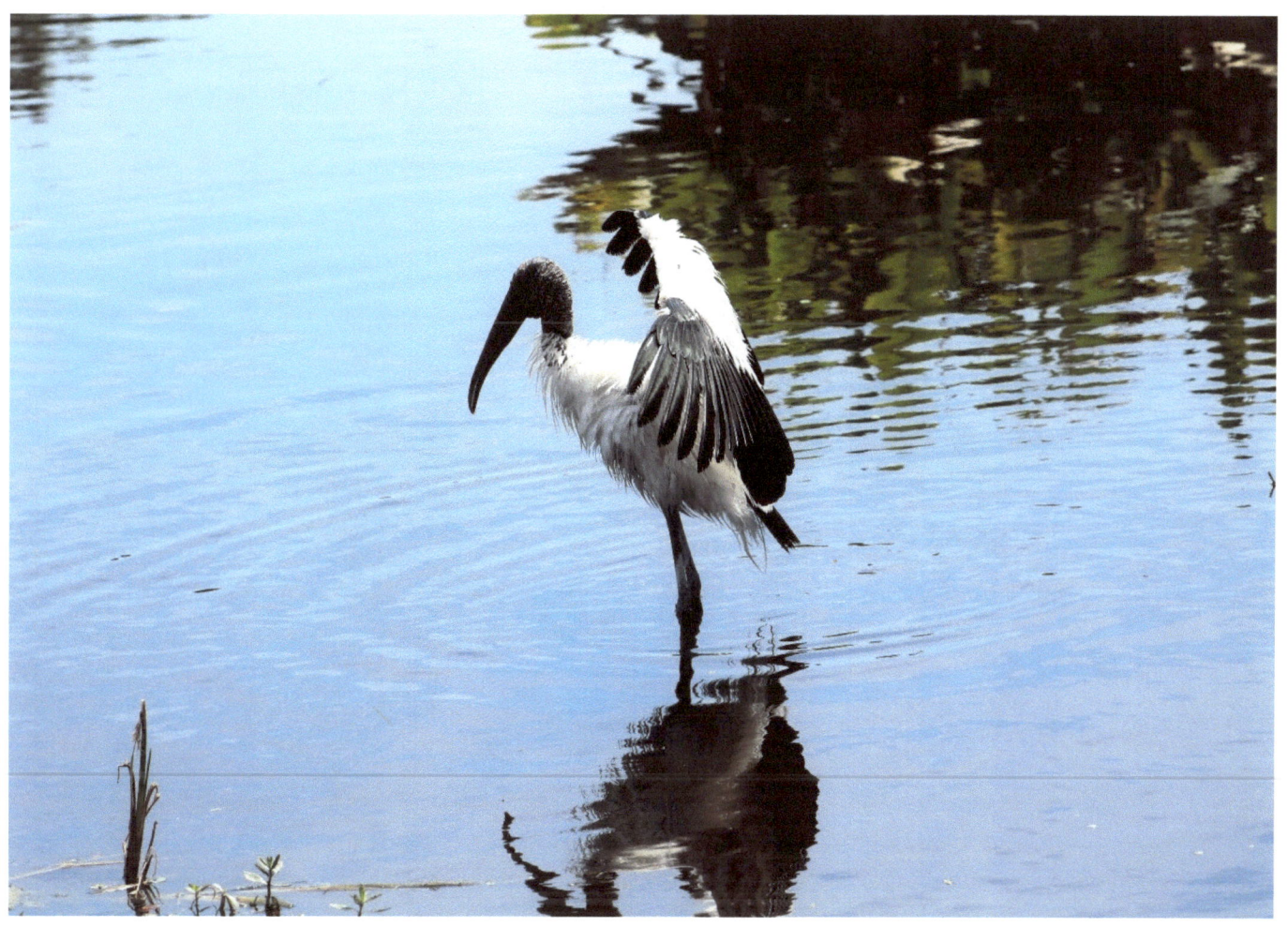

DANCING. Whether with a partner (left) or alone (above), wood storks lift their wings and balance their bodies to present graceful displays of elegance and poise. Their spread-wing posture can help the storks dry their feathers, regulate body temperature, and shade their eggs. This behavior is also a social display that may be used to relieve anxiety or assert strength. Each display is a chance for observers to catch a glimpse of the prismatic green and purple hues of the primary flight feathers.

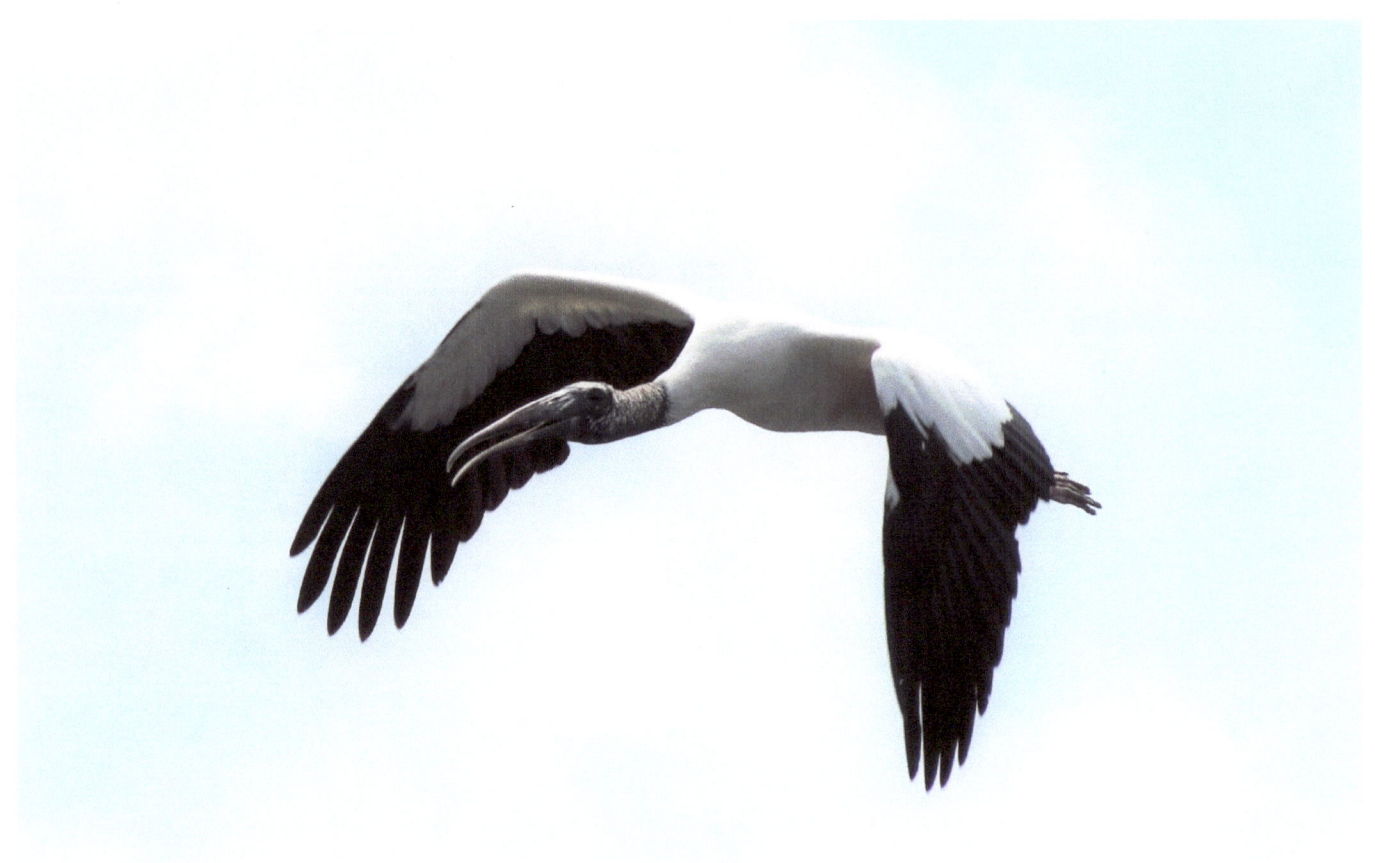

CONSERVATION. No longer listed as endangered, the status of the wood stork in the southeastern United States is currently Threatened. The human management of water levels, historically the greatest threat to the species, is today the greatest opportunity for its survival. Through coordination across agencies and efforts such as the Comprehensive Everglades Restoration Plan (CERP), the habitats that wood storks and countless other species need will be significantly expanded.

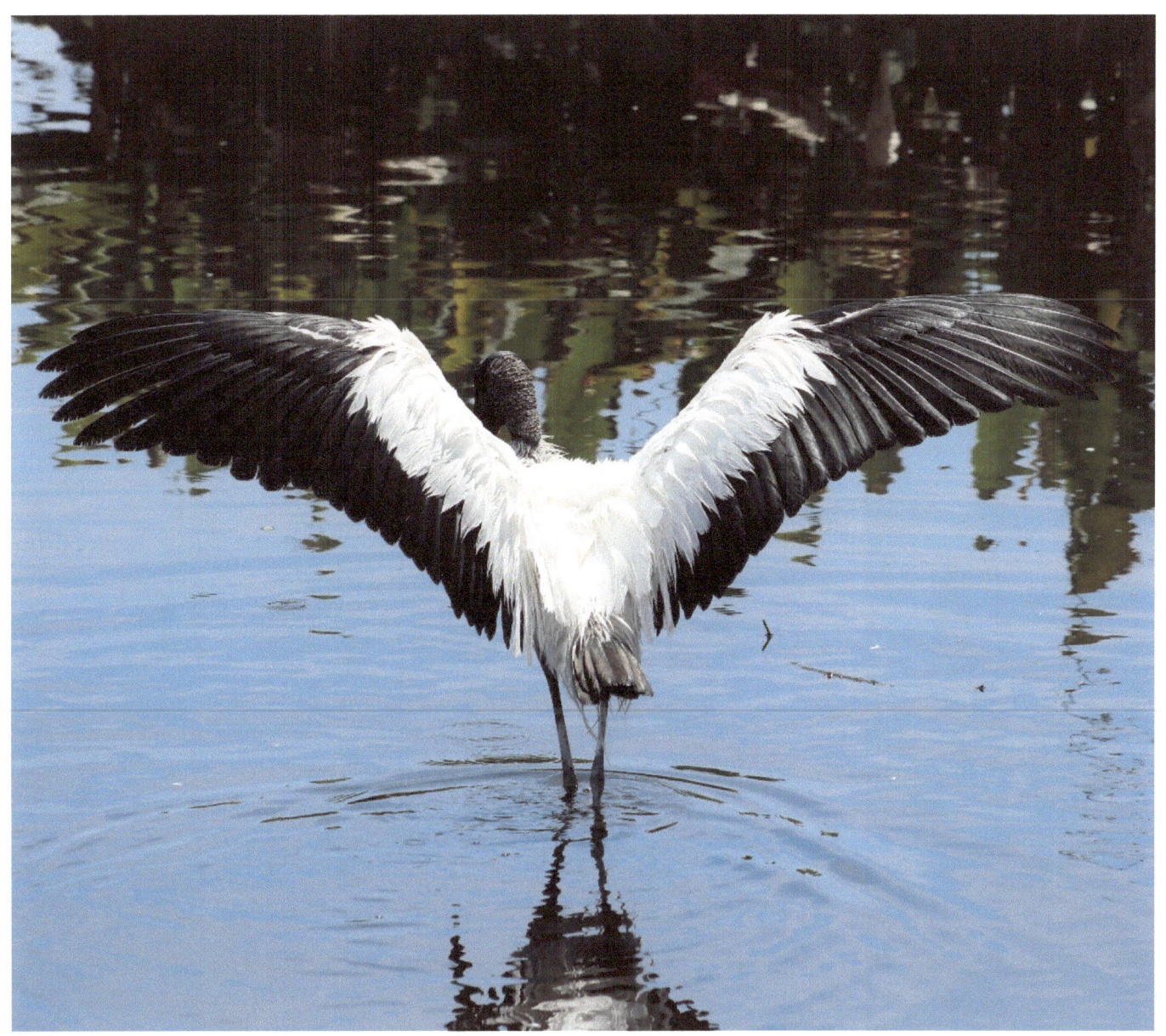

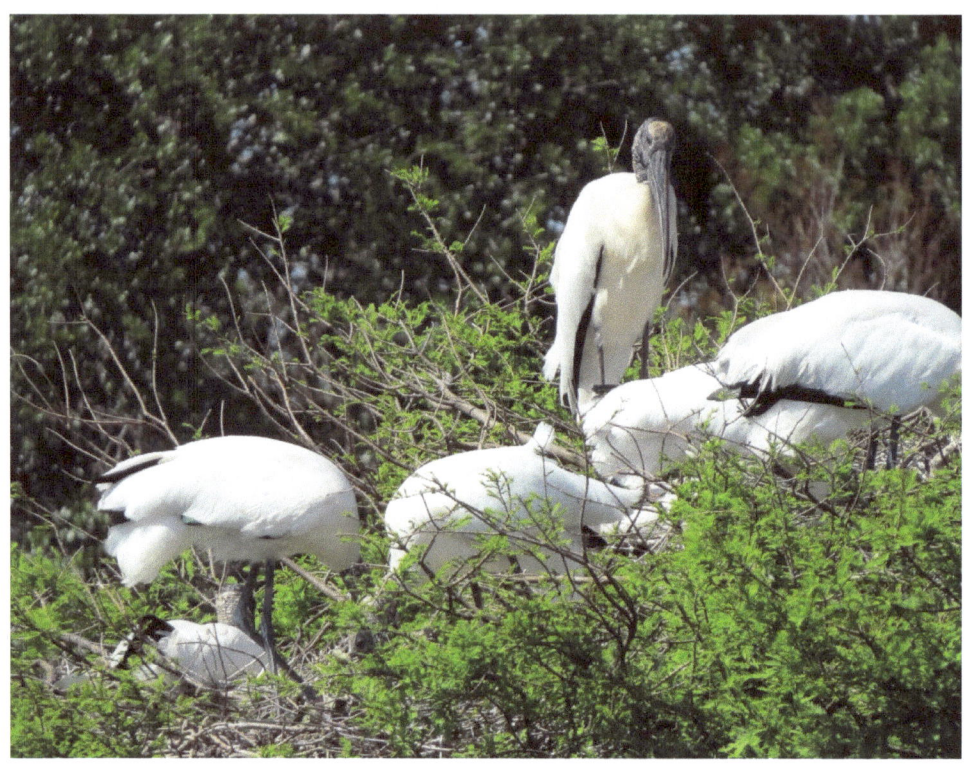

REFERENCES

Cornell Lab of Ornithology. "All About Birds: Wood Stork Overview." Cornell University, Last Modified 2017, https://www.allaboutbirds.org/guide/Wood_Stork

Florida Power & Light. "Florida's Wood Storks." Accessed August 4, 2018, https://www.fpl.com/environment.html

Kushlan, James A., and Frohring, Paula C. "The history of the southern Florida Wood Stork population." *The Wilson Bulletin* 98, No. 3 (1986): 368-386. https://sora.unm.edu/sites/default/files/journals/wilson/v098n03/p0368-p0386.pdf

U.S. Fish & Wildlife Service. "Species Profile for Wood stork (Mycteria americana)." Environmental Conservation Online System. Last modified 2014, https://ecos.fws.gov/ecp0/profile/speciesProfile?spcode=B06O

www.ingramcontent.com/pod-product-compliance
Lightning Source LLC
Chambersburg PA
CBHW051822210526
45473CB00005B/1699